To Ann, with best wishes Eileen
7/8/14

Men I Have
Known

Eileen M. Younghusband

Eileen Younghusband

Published by
Candy Jar Books
113-116 Bute Street,
Cardiff Bay, CF10 5EQ
www.candyjarbooks.co.uk

A catalogue record of this book is available
from the British Library

ISBN: 978-0-9571548-5-8

Printed and bound in the UK by
CPI Group (UK) Ltd,
Croydon, CR0 4YY

Contents

Acknowledgments

The publishers and I would like to thank the following for their permission to reprint material within this book: The Rosenbach Museum & Library; Neil Gaiman; *Caterer and Hotelkeeper*, Quercus Editions. Every reasonable effort has been made to contact the relevant copyright holders. We apologise to any copyright holder who has not been acknowledged and request that they should contact the publisher so that the necessary acknowledgement can be made in future editions.

Prologue

I have always preferred the company of men – I consider them a challenge.

Fate has led me on a journey from schoolgirl to author via au pair, trainee actuary, wartime Royal Air Force officer, hotelier, pig breeder and scrap-metal dealer. On the way, I have travelled widely and met many men from many backgrounds – military and business, TV and politics, academic and agricultural, art, music and literature. Some were fascinating, some repellent. There were intriguing men but also traitors, interesting peasants and friendly tycoons. I knew many of these men well and some only as a passing acquaintance. They have amused me and taught me; some have caused me anger; some have loved me; some helped me and others have hurt me. And now in my nineties, I am still meeting interesting men. Long may it continue!

I never imagined that I would meet a Major who would later govern a once British colony, who after a tyrannical reign would escape to Saudi Arabia. Nor that I would meet, on several occasions, a future prime minister as well as the great Winston Churchill. Now in my sunset days, I take a delight in recalling the men and my memories of them.

Introduction

I had not expected to write this book – it came about when I mentioned to my publishers that I was to give a talk to a group of local businessmen. I had spoken to them some time before about my work for the WAAF in the Filter Room, and had been invited to join them for lunch. I was entertained by around thirty interesting men, a most convivial occasion. After lunch they asked me if I would return to speak to them in the following year. I agreed readily, and their chairman asked what the subject of the next talk would be. Off the top of my head and after a couple of glasses of excellent wine, I rashly said, 'Men I have known!' Little did they know why that phrase had jumped into my head.

Shortly after the war, my husband and I became hoteliers and were given the job of managing an inn in the centre of Reading by the family brewers, Simonds and Sons Ltd. It wasn't a glamorous post: the inn's clientele consisted at the time of Irish workmen, who were building the local nuclear plant, and local prostitutes. There was even a shillelagh behind the bar for protection!

Intent on bringing about a change, we put up all the prices and decided to offer a limited lunchtime food service. Converting one of many Victorian bars – the Snug – into a snack bar, I needed to decorate it in style. From a nearby delicatessen merchant, I purchased a range of Italian delicacies and a collection of his salami sausages; long ones, short ones, curled ones, some wrapped in foil and some in decorative twine. I hung this collection from a rear shelf in a colourful and attractive display.

When we had our first visit from the area Catering Manager, no doubt bent on evaluating our abilities, he pointed to the pendulously decorated shelves, and asked, 'And what have we here?' I cast caution to the winds, and replied, 'Men I have known, Sir!' Fortunately, he had a great sense of humour – he laughed, and from that moment, we became friends.

So that was the title of my talk, recorded by Candy Jar Films, and destined eventually to be turned into a sometimes serious and sometimes tongue-in-cheek book. I hope it entertains you.

Growing Up

Harlow Frederick Le Croissette

My father was the eighth generation of a family of Huguenots who escaped from France in 1698, at the time of the Revocation of the Edict of Nantes and the subsequent persecution of the Protestants.

At the age of fifteen he trained for five years as an apprentice cabinet maker and joiner, receiving his indenture certificate on the 3 March 1906. He volunteered early in the First World War and joined the Royal Fusiliers as a despatch driver, serving in the Somme and at Passchendale and in 1917 he transferred to the newly formed Royal Flying Corps. This is when my interest in the RAF was born.

His was the first male influence on my life. I would remember him leaving home very early every morning taking advantage of the cheap workman's ticket on the tram to the furniture factory in Islington. He could turn his hand to everything from sweeping the chimney to re-soling my shoes. He would cut my hair and take me out in the garden when the sky was clear and show me the planets. He would help me with homework and he found time to teach the local Boys' Brigade gymnastics. He was industrious and fun, he was reliable and thrifty. He gave me my work ethic; he was the blueprint for my life.

Gilbert – My First Love

In the 1930s few schools were co-educational. However, I considered myself lucky living in London as both my primary and secondary school had mixed classes so I was never intimidated or ill at ease with the male of the species. I decided I liked boys and I had my first boyfriend when I was seven-years-old. His name was Gilbert, and he had ginger hair. I wrote him a poem, 'Sweetheart divine, will you be mine?' However this glorious relationship did not last very long. I pushed him over one day and he got tar on his socks. His mother banned him forthwith from any further contact with me.

At my grammar school, Southgate County, boys and girls mixed freely. Together we would go to Alexander Palace – known as Ally Pally – for weekly roller-skating sessions and then on our way home we would stop off at the Leg of Mutton pond for a little gentle canoodling – all fairly innocent, not going farther than a kiss and a cuddle and home by eight o'clock. I had been influenced by the local Baptist Church to remain a virgin until I married, a rule I rigidly obeyed for a long time. In retrospect, I am not convinced that was a good idea and often wonder what I missed.

George – A Girlhood Crush?

It was not until I was in the sixth form that I settled on an official boyfriend – George Duncan, the son of the local police inspector. George was gorgeous, tall and blond, a keen athlete with the additional attraction of a slight trace of a Scottish accent. He was a fine singer and took part in all the musical festivals we had each year. He was also a great cricketer. I was envied by my friends when I became the chosen one. We started going out when I was fifteen-years-old. We were inseparable. Two years later his father was moved to take over Staines police station. We were broken-hearted but though we were many miles apart, we did our utmost to meet as often as possible.

Born in the years after the First World War and growing up in an outer suburb of London, I had no idea how a second war would soon change so many lives, bringing together people who in normal times would never have the opportunity nor the desire to mix. But war would also shatter relationships and we would grasp at happiness even for a brief moment. George, my first love, was very special but would play a sad part in my life in future years.

T. B. Everard, M.A. Cantab

The revered headmaster of my grammar school, Southgate County, was a Member of the Royal College of Music and Licentiate of the Royal Academy of Music, as well as holding an M.A. degree from Cambridge University. He was an innovative educationalist and an imposing figure – clean-shaven with steel-grey hair – always wearing his academic gown and inspiring immediate respect. As a talented and keen musician, he formed and conducted an excellent school orchestra. He was the motivator of the many musical productions including the annual Gilbert and Sullivan opera. The orchestra also played in the annual music festival and daily at assembly. He had a memorable habit of always having one pair of spectacles perched on his head, whilst wearing another pair and waving a third pair in his hands!

Parents of children entering a grammar school in the 1930s had to sign an agreement that they would keep their children in education until they were sixteen-years-old. We felt privileged. These were the days when the normal age to enter the world of work was fourteen. Mr Everard announced on my first day of entry to the sacred precincts, 'There is no first form in this school. You will start in the second form and you will take the General Schools and Matriculation examinations in four years time. This will mean I then have at least one year to begin your education before you enter into the real world.'

We would have the choice in that final year of studying Science, Arts or Commerce. This was a revolutionary idea and no other school offered a similar plan. Nevertheless such was his leadership that the school obtained the highest matriculation results in the area and all students had an opportunity to specialise in a preferred subject, even if they were unable to stay until they were eighteen.

I elected to study Commerce and by the following May obtained

7

passes in the City and Guilds examinations; in shorthand to 140 words a minute, typing to 60 words a minutes; and most importantly accountancy and book-keeping up to preparation of profit-and-loss accounts and balance sheets – an incredible start for a business career in those days. These skills have stood me in great stead in every part of my life. Furthermore, we were taught the foundations of economics, commercial French and commercial German. We were introduced to the basics of banking, taken to the Law Courts and Council meetings and generally equipped to enter the commercial world. Moreover, we were taught to speak eloquently and clearly. If we should ever have to speak from the platform, there was a large notice telling us to:

SPEAK UP – SPEAK OUT AND SPEAK SLOWLY

Advice which should be given to everyone. I will continue to sing the praises of T.B. Everard to my dying day, he gave me the confidence to address groups of people ranging from politicians to businessmen, to keep control of my finances and to believe that everything was possible if you tried hard enough.

George Mitchell – An Introduction to Showbiz

I remember the tall seventeen-year-old prefect when I was in my first year at Southgate County School. He was already a talented pianist and played in the school orchestra. He began his singing career in the school choir. Who would have guessed that later he would give so much pleasure to so many with his choir known as the Black and White Minstrels?

He was to become the musical director of this show and lead it to nationwide success. It was first broadcast on radio and then, in June 1958, appeared on television. It very soon became popular and developed into a regular Saturday evening prime-time show. During the nine years that the show was broadcast in black and white, the singers' faces were blacked-up. This face make up was actually red as black did not film very well. Audiences regularly exceeded 18,000! The production gained considerable international kudos; in 1961, it won a Golden Rose at Montreux for the best light-entertainment programme and the first three albums of songs produced between 1960 and 1962 all did extremely well. However, in later years, the show began to be seen as offensive on account of the blackened faces of the white singers. It was regarded as stereotyping and a petition against it was received by the BBC in 1967. Later when it was presented without blacking-up, it was initially successful but finally ran out of steam. Despite his fame, he usually would turn up at school reunions, much to everyone's delight. Eventually George Mitchell emigrated to the United States.

Warren Mitchell – Till Death Us Do Part

He was another member of Southgate County School to reach the dizzy heights of fame. He had always taken part in school theatrical shows and later trained for an acting career. For many years he kept the nation laughing in the Cockney series, *Till Death Us Do Part*. I loved this programme, his character – a dogmatic old Cockney, a fierce Royalist and a true-blue Tory has gone down in history as one of the most watched programmes of its time. He played the indomitable Alf Garnett. Originally his name was Warren Misell and he arrived in my final year. He came from an immigrant Russian Jewish family. But when I knew him, he was a scruffy lad in the second form and of no importance to a sixth former. I remember he always took part in any entertainments that the school put on and showed a natural ability to act. Little did I realise how much he would add to the British comedy scene and how he would continue to act in many other roles for many more years.

René Cadier – Just a Passing Acquaintance I Thought!

In these early teenage years I had piano lessons every Saturday, despite never having much musical talent. During the summer I would meet many foreign students staying with my music teacher. One, Rene Cadier, became a brief friend for a fortnight. He was a good-looking, brown-haired sixteen-year-old with charming manners and laughing eyes.

He told me he came from Pau in the Pyrenees and he wanted to be a pilot. This stuck in my mind. When he returned home, I thought that was the last I would ever see of him. How wrong I was! I could never have imagined how he would reappear a few years later under very different circumstances – at a time when he had reached safety after a dangerous but exciting adventure – an adventure which could have led to his death.

Jack Rolfe – Making an Entrance

Jack Rolfe taught me German in my last two school years and was another memorable influence: he took over the class from R.V. Groves who had given up teaching to start the School Travel Service. His successor arrived straight from university, in his early twenties. I was the first pupil to meet him. This young, rather dishy male was at the entrance to the school as I arrived, not sure which door to take. I pointed him in the right direction. He was tall with thick blond hair and his leg was encased in a frame and bandages, due to a rugby injury.

I had no idea he was to be teaching me in his first class. We assembled for our German lesson. The boys, bent on playing a joke on the new teacher, grabbed my bathing costume, pinned it on the blackboard and drew a sexy body around it!

The new teacher arrived – it was the same young man I had just spoken with, accompanied by the Headmaster, who pointing to the blackboard said, 'To whom does this object belong?'

I reluctantly put up my hand, 'It is mine, sir.' I was duly and unfairly reprimanded until one of the boys admitted they were the ones responsible.

Once the class got under way, the new teacher asked me my name. I replied, 'Eileen Le Croissette'.

'Oh no,' he exclaimed in dismay, 'not another one of that family.' It seemed that he and my cousin Stanley had fallen out when both were students at London University – not an auspicious beginning. But things improved and he was responsible for my love of learning foreign languages. Later, in July 1939, he arranged for me to stay with his professor in Bonn in the Rhineland. I was thrilled when he came out on a visit to see me there and bought me my first glass of alcohol, *Apfelwasser*, a type of strong cider. Ten days after that visit, we were at war with Germany and he would be in the Army.

Werner Eisner – A Berliner and My Penfriend

As soon as I began to learn German, I acquired a penfriend. He lived in Berlin and was a couple of years older than I was. He always wrote in German. On leaving school, he began his training as a dentist. He never once mentioned politics but wrote about his love of music and his pet dog. His photo showed a dark-haired, serious-looking young man. I was certain he was not a Nazi and he never mentioned the *Hitler Jugend* but nevertheless, he like every young German had to complete those six months of compulsory work service called *Arbeitsdienst*. He wrote that he was helping to build motorways – and planting trees alongside the road. I doubt whether he realised that very soon these *Autostrassen* would be used to move vast columns of troops about to invade neighbouring countries or that the planting of trees had been planned to shield these movements from observation from the air.

The last letter I received from him arrived at my house on 3 September 1939, the day Britain declared war against Germany. In it, he wrote he had been called up to serve in the infantry. I found this strange and asked myself why a now fully qualified dentist was being sent to the infantry. That would be our last contact.

It was not until several months after peace was declared when we were able to receive letters once more from Germany that I learned what had happened to him. His mother wrote to my parents – a sad letter – asking if we had survived the war and continued, 'Werner was killed in 1940 at Arras... as cannon fodder'. None of us realised what this meant until in 1980 I decided to visit Berlin and meet his sister, hoping finally to learn the truth. Her name was Gertrud, known as Gea. I asked what her mother had meant by 'cannon fodder' and why he had been sent to the infantry. 'It seemed to me such a waste after all his training,' I said.

She replied with bitterness in her voice. 'We were labelled second-class citizens although we were Christians,' and explained that on one side of the family there was Jewish blood, not enough to wear the yellow star but enough to be despised by the Nazi establishment. 'He was sacrificed – put in the front line of the infantry, the first to be killed.' She continued, 'I too suffered – I was a trained nurse but when the Nazis came to power, I was not allowed to practice my profession. Instead they sent me to Auschwitz, not as a prisoner but as a clerk. I was made to keep the records of all the belongings taken from the Jewish prisoners. Daily I saw their suffering.'

She explained that the Nazis were meticulous in recording the name of every prisoner entering the camp. This was her job as they arrived at the death camps. She was made to list every detail of the possessions taken from these doomed victims – jewellery, books – everything they brought with them, except what they stood up in.

Recently the nephew of Werner and Gea made contact with me and the German connection is once more restored.

Dangerous Times

Monsieur Marcel Boucher – A French Deputé from Alsace

R.V. Groves (I never did know his first name) was my original German teacher but he left the school in 1935 to start his own business. He remains in my memory as an angular man with a long nose and a habit of pulling at his ear.

He made his name and his fortune pioneering school foreign exchange programmes, now such a common event but in the 1930s a novel experience. He founded the School Travel Service – STS – and it was through him that the course of my life was changed when I was almost seventeen. At the time, I was working in the cash department of a large life assurance company, the Scottish Provident Institution, travelling daily to the heart of London. It was a pretty boring job and as a female, I was treated very much as an inferior. Whilst the young men of the same age came dressed in smart suits and ties, I was made to wear a horrible scratchy mauve overall which did nothing for my sex appeal.

When in 1938, Mr Groves wrote to my parents asking if I would be interested in joining him in his new venture, I was all for it – anything to get out of the daily train journey, jammed into overfull carriages. He knew I was fairly proficient in both French and German. His new business was growing rapidly and the idea was to train me to travel around France and Germany planning school exchanges. But, he insisted, I must first spend six months in each country to perfect my knowledge of both these languages. Amazingly my parents agreed. I suppose they felt they could trust me to cope. It was left to us to find an au pair position in France to give me an opportunity of living with a French family. Searching in *The Lady* magazine, famous for its respectable advertisements, we found a French family looking for someone to teach their three children English. This seemed the ideal opportunity. I applied; I wrote a letter in my best French accompanied by two references, one from the Minister of the Baptist Church and one from my old Headmaster.

They answered by return of post, saying they would be happy to welcome me to the family. There would be no salary but they would pay for my travel and all my expenses whilst with them. I was to stay initially for six months. But to my surprise, the letter came from the office of a Deputy in the Chamber of Deputies, the French Parliament.

In May, two months after my seventeenth birthday, I was on my way. I travelled alone by train from London to Paris and then on a further train to Contrexéville. The journey was fascinating: beautiful scenery, different food and a chance to practise my French.

Monsieur Boucher, my host, had been a mayor of this Alsace town in the Vosges Mountains, close to the border with Germany. During his tenure, he had successfully built the town's reputation as a spa with health-giving springs and it was now a fashionable place for rich Parisians to take the waters, bringing increased prosperity to the populace. Due to his success, he had later been elected to represent the region of the Vosges in the Chamber of Deputies. I would later learn that he was also the President of the Compagnons de Jeanne d'Arc. This French heroine was born in the Vosges region, in the nearby town of Domrémy. I was not then aware that many of the Deputies who supported it at that time were all of centre or right-wing persuasion despite Les Compagnons officially showing no political bias.

I was met at the station by Madame Boucher, in an enormous chauffeur-driven Mercedes and taken to a beautiful house in wooded grounds on the outskirts of this attractive town. My new host met me at the door. 'Bienvenue,' he said. 'Welcome to the family.' He was an elegant man, dressed formally and speaking impeccable French.

At first, I was a little anxious. Could I cope? Were my clothes suitable for this type of life? But before many days passed, I relaxed and felt like part of the family. From the beginning, I was treated as one of them. I spent the daytime teaching the children English but each evening I joined Monsieur and Madame Boucher at dinner when we dressed appropriately for the occasion. I would meet many of his political colleagues and important businessmen. It was a little overwhelming at first but, as my French improved, so did my confidence. So it was that I met the newly elected Romanian Prime Minister, Miron Cristea. He was a balding old man with a lived-in face and a massive beard. He had taken office in the previous February after the sudden death of his predecessor and, I later learned, was considered anti-Semitic.

During the meal, we would always converse in French. On this evening Monsieur Cristea turned to me and said with a strong Teutonic accent, 'Your French is far better than mine.' This surprised me since I had been told that Romanian was a Latin-based language. But it also delighted me as it meant that my efforts to become more fluent were succeeding. It was some time later that I learnt he came from an Austro-Hungarian background and French was an acquired language. He was pleasant enough but, I believe, considered a mere puppet under the control of King Carol ll. Fortunately we did not get into politics during dinner but instead enjoyed a great meal which finished with the famous dessert croquembouche which I noticed he devoured heartily.

My stay in France was not to last very long. As a politician, Monsieur Boucher was aware of the threat of war. He had served with honour in the First World War, gaining a military decoration and he was now a Reservist Officer in Les Chasseurs, one of the regional Infantry regiments. In August he was summoned to report for duty. He certainly looked the part in his uniform. I learned he had been sent to camp on the banks of the Rhine. On the far side lay Germany and the demilitarised zone. The German army, despite the restrictions imposed at the armistice of 1918, had set up an illegal military encampment on the opposite of the river, which they had mined. It was obvious Hitler was preparing for war. Europe was facing what would be known as the Munich Crisis. Monsieur Boucher realised the dangers and phoned home, insisting I return to Britain at once. It was August and I had only been in France for three months. My dreams of a career in the travel business were shattered.

The journey home was long and difficult. The trains were crowded with refugees. I had to spend a night in Paris and on the journey to Calais I shared a carriage with terrified Jewish families, escaping threatening Nazi retribution. There was fear written over their faces. I was sad to leave the Boucher family and I had no idea at that time how their lives would soon change dramatically. Nor did I know of the divided loyalties of the people of Alsace, situated so close to the border of Germany.

The Office Worker – My Forgotten Companion

So it was back to working in London once more, this time with a paper agency. I was the only female in an office of men. I formed a special friendship with one of them, a young clerk. He wasn't handsome but had an interesting face, slightly foreign-looking, I thought. We found a common bond in our love for poetry. We would attempt to write soul-searching poems and during our lunch break, we would sit on the banks of the River Thames, eating our packed lunches, reading our latest efforts to each other and comparing notes. At the age of eighteen, we were both very serious and intense and wanting to put the world to rights. For me it was a purely non-sexual friendship. I will never know how he felt, for it was to come to a sudden end when he was called up as war was declared. All I have to remember him is the letter he left me. It was headed, 'On Saying Goodbye' and continued: 'Twenty-four hours from now and all the goodbyes will have been said. Goodbye – what an expression! It is said with such a variety of feelings – the goodbye you just let fall after a casual meeting in a pub or after a few hours journey on a train. Goodbye has no real meaning then – it's just the thing to say and people expect it.

Then there's the goodbye you say at the end of a long period at a school, or on a camp when posted. It brings a feeling of sorrow for a few hours as one realises that you are leaving behind friends you've made, associations you will miss; but not for long, for as new associations are formed, the old ones are soon forgotten. Now the real goodbye is different. And the one I say today will be that. It will convey all the meaning of the other goodbyes and much more. The word will be the same but the feeling will be so much deeper. I have no illusions as to whether we will meet again, but in the forming of new associations there is one I shall never forget – I just can't. So to me this goodbye will mean more than the mere act of parting. To quote Lamartine again: "*Une seule être me manquera et le monde sera depeuplé*" – "One sole person I will miss and the world will seem empty."'

I would never hear from him again, never know what happened to him. And now, I cannot even remember his name.

George Again

After leaving school at sixteen, George and I had continued to meet whenever possible. He was better looking than ever and now six foot tall – every girl's dream. When I left for France we both wondered whether this was a permanent parting. He consoled himself by joining the rowing club, making new friends. He spent a lot of time practising with his crew on the Thames.

On my forced return from France, George and I met again and it was as if we had never been parted. We both realised how much we meant to each other. But I was not to see him very often. He was now training as a surveyor and constantly busy and travelling to Staines became increasingly difficult.

When he was seventeen, at the time of the Munich Crisis, he had joined the Territorial Army. A year later, he was called up for service, a month before war was declared. By then I was back working for the

Scottish Provident Institution once more. By the autumn of 1940, the bombing in London was intense and the damage in the city enormous. The company decided to evacuate to Woking. I was now living and working in a large house on the outskirts of the town. George had finished his training and was already with the British Expeditionary Force in France and had been transferred to the Military Police.

By the spring the Germans had broken through the Maginot Line and had invaded France. I anxiously waited for news but none came. Soon after arriving in Woking, I was spending any spare time I had working with the YMCA canteen, catering for the many troops in the area. The war was going badly, we were in retreat. At the end of May our forces were gathering at Dunkirk for evacuation. The struggle to get our men back to Britain would last until the 4th of June. The retreat became an unexpected victory.

René Cadier Reappears

The returning troops from the beaches of France who were fit to travel were moved immediately away from where they landed and into trains, as it was impossible to cope with so many at the ports. Woking station was one of their first stops where they would get food and something to drink. I was given permission to work with the YMCA canteen there all through the day as well as in the evenings. Trains were arriving every half hour, full of weary men in torn and bloodied uniforms. Many of the soldiers were injured, all were hungry. They stayed no more than a quarter of an hour, time enough to get a cup of tea and pick up some sandwiches and then they were off once more. It was heart-wrenching to see these remnants of our army. But at least these men were home.

Then on the third day, I was standing behind the table, handing out sandwiches and pouring tea into paper cups, when I heard someone shout, '*Mon Dieu, c'est* Eileen!' There, in front of me, was a young man in a French Air Force uniform wearing pilot's wings. I looked again and couldn't believe my eyes. It was René Cadier, older, grey-faced and haggard but the same René I had known when I was fourteen, and he was a student visiting my home town. As I turned towards him, he gave me the warm enticing smile I remembered. It was hard to believe that of all the places we could meet again, it was here on a railway station, as he was fleeing his homeland.

Our time together was brief but he explained how he had managed to escape. He had flown his aircraft until it ran out of fuel then he had crash-landed and destroyed the plane, together with all his records. After a while he joined up with some retreating British troops, finally reaching the beaches and rescue. I gave him a large pack of sandwiches and a quick drink. Within a very short time, he was ordered back on the train. He hugged me, we were both crying. I wished him well and then he was gone.

Many years later I saw him one more time. On a journey through France in 2003, on my way to Spain, I drove through the Pyrenees. Seeing a sign to the town of Pau, I remembered René had once told me that was where he lived. I found a telephone directory and there was his name and address. So I went to the house and knocked on the door. He answered it and instantly recognised me. We had a brief but emotional reunion. He told me he was now a civilian pilot with Air France.

However, that is not the end of the story. Recently I told a French author, Geneviève Moulard, about meeting him in such circumstances and she offered to search through the Air Force records to find his history. There we learned that after Dunkirk he volunteered to return to France to join the Resistance and worked in the Pyrenees, aiding escaping pilots and refugees making their way into Spain and safety. Rejoining the Air Force after the war, he had later become the most famous pilot with the civilian airline, Air France, having flown every one of their aircraft on every route they covered. He too had written a book.

George – The Escape

Like so many others, during those days of the Dunkirk rescue, I had waited for news of a loved one, always fearing the worst. One morning there was a short phone call from George's father, saying his son was back in Britain and convalescing. Another wait of days and finally a letter arrived from George saying he was being posted but he did not know where. He never mentioned Dunkirk or how he escaped. It would be much longer before I learned of his leadership and bravery on the beaches there.

During the evacuation, the Military Police were ordered to man the beaches and organise the transfer of the troops to waiting vessels as they arrived. Most of these vessels were anchored offshore. George came across a large rowing boat on the beach he was patrolling, complete with two sets of oars. He called to a fellow Staff Sergeant from the Police Corps and together they manned this small craft, ferrying groups of soldiers out to a waiting freighter. They did this journey eight times, constantly under intense shelling and Stuka attack. The boat, overfilled with survivors, was a heavy load to steer and on the last trip, George collapsed with exhaustion. The skipper of the freighter took one look at these two men who had saved so many others and ordered, 'Stop now, you have done enough. Get aboard.' George and his fellow oarsman were hauled aboard the freighter and they headed for home.

It would be months before I had any letters from him. The first one arrived in the form of an airgraph – all letters from the Army overseas came in this form. These were photo reproductions of troop's mail home. Letters were too bulky to send other than by boat so they were photographed and the negatives sent home by air, where they were developed and sent on to the families. I knew then he must have been sent abroad and since we were opening a second front in the Middle East, I assumed that was where he was. I let him know I was now in the Air Force. Then one day another airgraph arrived asking if I would to marry him. We had been sweethearts for so long; I did not hesitate in writing back to say yes. We announced our engagement. I was ecstatic with happiness.

His address was given as 7th Armoured Division – known as the 'Desert Rats'. I followed the news from the Middle East daily. After the first battle of El Alamein, it seemed our troops had been repelled. Things were not going well. More weeks passed with occasional letters. Finally the War Office decided a change in command was needed. General Montgomery took over the Eighth Army and the situation immediately improved. The second battle of El Alamein brought news of the defeat of Rommel and the German army. Then George's letters stopped. I had visions of him being wounded in the battle or perhaps killed. I was desperate to know but I was unable to contact any of his family as his father had recently died, his brother had been called up and his sister had moved away.

Three months passed before a letter in an unknown hand arrived at my home. It was signed Mary Duncan, George's sister. I feared the worst.

My mother forwarded it to me. His sister wrote to say that George was now married! His wife was an ATS signals operator whom he had met in Cairo. It seems he had been injured in the advance on El Alamein and during his convalescence, he had met her. Obviously they swiftly became more than friends and she found herself pregnant. She was immediately discharged from the Army and was now living with Mary, awaiting the birth of their child. I was shocked, hurt and angry that he had not had the courage to write to me himself. It would not be until 1985 before I would hear from him once more.

Eric Padfield – My Cousin

A few months after Dunkirk, I decided I must do more for my country than work in an office and serve cups of tea at the YMCA. My favourite cousin, Eric, had joined the RAF before the war and after being awarded the Lord Wakefield Scholarship, he was sent to the Officers' Flying

School at RAF Cranfield where he trained as a pilot. Since the outbreak of war, he had been teaching new recruits to fly. In June 1940, during one of the training flights when they had taken off in bad weather, there had been a tragic accident and the aircraft crashed in the mountains in Scotland. The trainee pilot and my cousin died instantly.

Since my father had transferred from the Army in 1917 to the newly formed Royal Flying Corps, there was no doubt in my mind that I too must follow their example and, early in 1941, I volunteered for service with the Women's Auxiliary Air Force.

Royal Air Force Days

Sir Robert Watson-Watt

When the WAAF enrolling officer learned I had excelled in mathematics, I was informed that I would be trained as a Clerk Special Duties. When I asked what this entailed, I was told, 'You will first sign the Official Secrets Act and then you will find out.' This was my introduction to the secret world of Radar. My later technical training as a Filterer Officer took place at Bawdsey Manor in Suffolk, the centre of Radar's development. This isolated manor house stands at a prominent position near the mouth of the River Deben, on the other side of the river from Felixstowe. It was here that the Chain Home Radar system was developed. During our three weeks of intensive training, we would meet the man, Robert Watson-Watt, considered by many to be the inventor of RDF (Range and Direction Finding). This system provided the vital advance information that helped the Royal Air Force win the Battle of Britain. After graduating with a Bachelor of Science from the University of Dundee, Watson-Watt specialised in the study of radio, or 'wireless telegraphy' as it was then known, and also the physics of radio-frequency oscillators and wave propagation.

In the early 1930s, it was rumoured Germany was building a 'death ray' to be used against aircraft. Watson-Watt was asked to build a version of this for our own defence system. Working together with his team of scientists and engineers, it was found impossible to construct but he put forward the idea of detection by radio waves. Thus RDF, later to become Radar, was created to give advance warning of enemy aircraft approaching our coasts. Watson-Watt was a man of great imagination and much of his success in management came from his ability to cut corners and get things done speedily.

We would see him occasionally when he would come in to check how our training was getting on and he would ask whether there was any particular aspect we found difficult. He was middle-aged and slightly balding with a round face and glasses. He always wore a humorous expression, but we regarded him with awe. The invention of Radar, coupled with the Dowding System, introduced by the Air Chief Marshall Sir Hugh Dowding, ensured our air supremacy, foiling Operation Sea Lion and leading to Hitler abandoning thoughts of invasion and instead opening a second front against Russia.

The first Filter Room under the Dowding System was constructed at Bawdsey Manor but just before the beginning of war, it was moved to Fighter Command Headquarters at Stanmore, Middlesex. Watson-Watt was a frequent visitor there, checking on its operation together with his team of scientists, the only people who were not in uniform.

It was rumoured Watson-Watt had a great sense of humour. The Watson-Watt Society of Brechin reports that in later years, when he visited Canada, he was pulled over for speeding by a radar-gun toting policeman. His comment to the officer was, 'Had I known what you were going to do with it I would never have invented it!' He wrote an ironic poem – 'Rough Justice' – about the incident afterwards:

Pity Sir Robert Watson-Watt,
Strange target of this Radar plot.
And thus, with others I can mention
The victim of his own invention
His magical all-seeing eye
Enabled cloud-bound planes to fly
But now by some ironic twist
It spots the speeding motorist
And bites, no doubt, with legal wit,
The hand that once created it.
[Courtesy of the Watson-Watt Society of Brechin]

He would later marry the Air Chief Commandant of the Women's Auxiliary Air Force, Dame Katherine Trefusis Forbes, having met her at Bentley Priory. This was the man whose ingenuity and leadership saved Britain from invasion and changed the face of history.

Air Chief Marshal Hugh Dowding, 1st Baron Dowding of Bentley Priory GCB GCVO CMG

'A difficult man, a self-opinionated man, a most determined man, and a man who knew more than anybody about all aspects of aerial warfare.' This was Sir Frederick Pile's description of Lord Hugh Dowding. He was known to us as 'Stuffy' and as the man who prevented Adolf Hitler from achieving air supremacy, causing him to abandon Operation Sea Lion and the invasion of Britain.

Hugh Dowding served for over forty years in the Royal Air Force, initially as a pilot in the First World War. He became the commanding officer of RAF Fighter Command in the years prior to the Second World War and was promoted Air Marshal and knighted in 1937. He disagreed with the Prime Minister Stanley Baldwin's 1932 declaration that 'the bomber will always get through.' His conviction that this was wrong inspired him to develop the Dowding System – the integrated defence system combining Radar, the Observer Corps of human observers with raid plotting and the radio control of aircraft. He instigated a complex telephone communication system, buried underground. This system was the heart of our air defence.

The first Filter Room under the Dowding System was constructed at Bawdsey Manor in Suffolk where Watson-Watt had done the initial work on RDF. Just before the beginning of war, it was moved to Fighter Command Headquarters at Bentley Priory, Stanmore, Middlesex. Eventually there were seven Filter Rooms, covering the whole of Britain's coastal air defence. His contribution to Britain's victory in the air will soon be commemorated in a heritage museum.

He was revered by all who served under him. He would always

identify himself with his pilots and fought for the Fighter aircraft to be equipped with bulletproof wind shields. His contribution to ensuring Britain was never invaded by the enemy is incalculable. Although I only saw him on two occasions during my training at Bawdsey, his influence was felt throughout all the days of my service.

Wing Commander Sydney Rudd

Among the many specialist RAF officers I would meet after initial training was Wing Commander Rudd, the officer in charge of 10 Group Filter Room at Rudloe Manor, Box. He was a pre-war officer, having been promoted from the ranks. He ruled with a rod of iron but unlike many of the male officers, realised the potential of the airwomen under his control. Anyone showing mathematical ability and spatial awareness was recommended for promotion. He demanded high standards but was prepared to recognise hard work and ability. It was thanks to him that within three months of becoming a Filter plotter, I was recommended for a commission to train as a Filterer officer. He would later be transferred to Fighter Command headquarters during my time there and I would renew my acquaintance with him and often babysit for the family on official occasions.

Squadron Leader Daniel Meinerzthagen

After four weeks' training at Bawdsey Manor, I was posted to 9 Group Filter Room at Preston as a Section Officer where I came under the command of Squadron Leader Daniel Meinertzthagen. He was a member of a banking family which rivalled the Rothschilds at one stage although his father was an Army officer and considered a controversial figure. He served abroad in Africa and India and was in British Intelligence in the First World War. Daniel Meinerzthagen was tall and autocratic and difficult to work with. He had little time for the minor ranks of officers, especially the women. I worked under him for about six months and was always glad when he was not the duty controller. However, one evening watch will always remain in my memory.

Information came through that a special operation had been carried out successfully. The well-known Radio Fécamp had been taken over by the German army as a Radar station. Our special forces had successfully landed there, captured a German scientist and destroyed the station. Instead of showing delight at the success of the operation, he was most irate, calling out, 'My father owned Radio Fécamp, what right had they in destroying it without asking his permission!' I could not believe what I had heard but that was typical of the man. We all felt that he considered himself and his family vastly superior to anyone else.

Sir Winston Churchill

It was while I was stationed at Preston, that we tracked an aircraft approaching from the west. It was not showing the signal IFF – identification friend or foe. Since it was not usual to see hostiles in that area, the duty Controller designated it an X raid, meaning of doubtful identity. This was my first contact with Winston Churchill – over the air and from a great distance. He was travelling in this aircraft, returning from a meeting with President Roosevelt in the United States. It was only when it was about forty miles off the west coast, the pilot realised his error and turned on the IFF signal. In time we redesignated the track as friendly.

Later I had the pleasure of seeing Churchill often at Stanmore when he would wander into the Fighter Command Filter Room. He would look over the balcony, taking in everything that was happening – his visits would always be when the table was busy with a special operation. Once the V1 bombardment started, he was a frequent visitor, checking on how we were managing to cope. Since we were always very busy during his visits, sadly this was the nearest I got to this great man; watching him as he stood on the balcony above us, usually with an unlit cigar in his mouth.

The Men at 10 Group – Actors, Aviators and All Sorts

In the spring of 1942, I was posted again to 10 Group at Rudloe Manor, near Bath. There we had a joint male and female Officers' Mess. Many of the women were still under twenty, a large number of them from girls' public schools. Their upbringing had not allowed them many opportunities to mix with men and they found it rather intimidating since most of the male officers were quite a bit older. Fortunately my wider experience gave me some advantage.

Air Vice Marshall Augustus Orlebar had been both an Army officer and later a Royal Air Force officer and had served in both World Wars, gaining a CBE, an AFC and Bar. Between the wars he was involved in high-speed flying, competing in the Schneider Trophy and holding the world air-speed record. In July 1941, he became the Air Officer Commanding 10 Fighter Group and later in 1943, Deputy Chief of Combined Operations. He was an inspiring leader and we all worshipped him.

Rudloe Manor was not an operational Fighter station so there were not many young pilots to amuse us. However, when fighter pilots were on a rest period they were sent to the group headquarters to learn about Radar. Amongst the air aces I would meet in the Mess was 'Cat's Eyes' Cunningham, the famous night fighter pilot who had downed twenty enemy aircraft. His nickname of Cat's Eyes came from the cover-up explanation for his success during these night raids. It was claimed a special group of British pilots ate carrots in order to develop superior night vision. This romantic, but unbelievable, explanation for his success, masked the reality. British scientists had secretly developed a sophisticated and formidable airborne radar system which allowed its pilots to home in on Luftwaffe bomber streams, often with devastating consequences. Radar equipment used for night flying was called A.I. – air interception. It is rumoured Cunningham himself, a self-effacing and modest individual, detested his nickname.

Another of the pilots who spent time with us there was a young

Scotsman, Edward Mortimer-Rose, who was always the leader of any mad event which occurred in the Mess. His favourite game was to start a competition of diving through the hatch of the bar and seeing how far you could go – usually carried out after a particularly boozy evening and often with dire effects.

He joined the RAF in April 1039 and posted to 234 Squadron in November 1939. He was involved in many air combats and awarded a DFC for service during the Battle of Britain and in the following months after shooting down many enemy aircraft, later receiving a Bar to this award. The citation reads, 'This officer has displayed great skill as a fighter pilot. In a recent combat he destroyed two of five enemy aircraft destroyed by his flight thus bringing his victories to at least six. He has set a splendid example and has contributed materially to the high standard of efficiency in his squadron.'

After a rest period with us at Rudloe, he was posted to Malta, commanding 249 Squadron. Later in the Middle East, he was seriously injured manning ground defence guns at Hal Far airfield during a bombing raid. He then transferred to 111 Squadron. Sadly in January 1943, he was killed in a flying accident with his squadron in Tunisia and buried in the Medjez-El-Bab War Cemetery. He had over ten enemy aircraft to his name and was still only twenty-two-years-old.

Rex Harrison

Amongst the older officers were some already famous people, including several from the entertainment world. The most famous was Rex Harrison. He was then a Flight Lieutenant in Air Raid Warnings Liaison Section and would frequently work on the same watch as us. He was very handsome, and always immaculate in his uniform but very haughty.

At that time Rex Harrison was married to Colette Thomas but carrying on an intense affair with Lilli Palmer, a German actress he had worked with previously. She was from a German Jewish family who had escaped to France in 1933. It was impossible for us not to know of this affair since each evening he would call Lilli on the phone in the anteroom. It was not a large room and as we sat drinking our coffee, we could not help overhearing all his conversation, which was usually pretty explicit. Early in 1943 he would divorce his first wife and marry Lilli. That marriage lasted fourteen years. He would then go on to marry a further two women.

When he was on duty on B watch, we would often have breakfast together. But I really couldn't fancy him, his table manners put me off; he would take a bite of his toast and, as he chewed, the sodden bread would ooze out of the side of his mouth. He never mixed with other officers, taking little part in the camp activities and had a reputation of being difficult to work with.

On one occasion, Peter Hoare, a Sergeant in the Entertainment Section, put on a production of *French without Tears*, a play in which Harrison had had a great success in before the war. We had some good amateur actors on the camp and they gave up their free time to provide entertainment for their colleagues. I was given a very small part as the French maid. Rex Harrison wandered in to a rehearsal once day, stayed for about five minutes, looked scathingly at our efforts, made no comment and left. Peter Hoare would later make his name as a much respected theatrical producer.

It would be at Rudloe that I would first meet Kenneth Horne who was a Squadron Leader and married to Jo, one of our Filterer Officers. Sadly, she left him and went off with a glamorous Polish fighter pilot from the nearby base at Colerne. But I would meet Kenneth again.

Kenneth Horne and Much-Binding-in-the-Marsh

Early in 1943 I had been posted to Fighter Command Headquarters at Bentley Priory, Stanmore. Kenneth was then officer in charge of the Balloon Command Unit stationed near us at Stanmore. He would often be present when we were invited to parties in the male Officers' Mess and, before long, he and I became good friends.

Later he was posted to Whitehall in the Equipment Branch. Soon after his arrival there, he invited me to join him for dinner on my next day off-duty. At the first opportunity, I called in to the Whitehall office where he worked, and made my way to his room on the second floor. On the door the notice read – Wing Commander G. Armitage, Wing Commander K. Horne and Squadron Leader R. Murdoch. I knocked and entered. The three men were busy doing *The Times* cryptic crossword – they were sitting around a large table, laughing and joking as they read out the clues and suggested the answers. I felt I was entering a performance. This was where Kenneth and Dickie Murdoch first met and where they worked on some of the funniest programmes of the times.

Kenneth was then in his late thirties, fairly tall and broad and already balding. He looked like the typical successful businessman, as he was in civilian life. Despite having had a rather unsuccessful academic career, he had been Sales Director with Triplex Glass and would later take over Chad Valley toys. He was one of the kindest of men and would do anything to help people.

When I first visited him in London, he and Dickie Murdoch were already planning the programme, *Much-Binding-in-the-Marsh*. He asked me to give him some idea of how WAAF would behave when they were all together and off-duty. I told him some of the more amusing occasions that I could remember from my days as an airwoman second class. He assured me they would introduce them in future programmes.

I met Kenneth several times after that and often went to his flat above the Lyons Corner House near Marble Arch. There were never any amorous moments and I often wonder if this is why his first and second wife left him. However, he was always interesting and witty and a kind and charming companion. I really enjoyed our friendship. Later when he appeared on *Monday Night at Eight* for the BBC, he invited me to several of the shows. As with so many wartime friendships, peacetime brought changes and contacts were lost.

Alvar Liddell – Plotter cum Newsreader

In the RAF at that time, we would meet and work with many famous people from broadcasting and the theatre but also from industry and the business world. Ronnie Squires, then a well-known actor on the London stage and John Myers, the film producer, both served with us as Controllers. It was a delight to hear their well-honed voices identifying the tracks on the Filter table, 'Make that a fighter and raid 234 a hostile.'

The distinguished BBC announcer, Alvar Liddell was for a short time one of our plotters. To hear his wonderful voice repeating the radar plot positions was an equal surprise. He was a very quiet man and one of the few male plotters in the Filter Room. I think he was overwhelmed by all the airwomen surrounding him. He went on to become an Intelligence Officer, spending some time at Bletchley Park.

Born in London of Swedish parents, he joined the BBC and became their chief announcer in 1937. It was during the Second World War that the BBC named its previously anonymous announcers and newsreaders to distinguish them from enemy propagandists. 'Here is the News, and this is Alvar Liddell reading it' became an inadvertent catchphrase. He made many historic broadcasts, including the announcement of the abdication of King Edward VIII. It was his voice we all heard on 3rd September 1939 when he read the ultimatum to Germany from 10 Downing Street and then at 11 a.m. introduced Neville Chamberlain as he told the nation that we were at war.

Post-war, he was appointed chief announcer for The Third Programme and he finally retired from the BBC in 1969. He later recorded over 237 volumes of Books for the Blind. I have always been one of his fans.

Augustus John and Dylan Thomas – Wartime London

Among the officers who worked with me in the Filter Room was Zoe

Hicks, reputedly an offspring of Augustus John. He had always been interested in 'gypsies' and would eventually set up home together with his wife and Zoe's supposed mother in a caravan. Zoe was herself an exotic figure and had many admirers. She went on to become a well-known actress after the war. She certainly had a close relationship with the Welsh artist and she would take selected groups of us to meet him in London in various hotel bars.

Augustus John's frequent companion at the time was Dylan Thomas and on a couple of occasions I was included in the invitation to join them. They were contrasting figures. Dylan Thomas, then in his mid-thirties, was charming but always untidy-looking and badly dressed, with ruffled curly hair. He was renowned for never paying his way in the pubs. I recall being shocked by his profanities and swearing. It is hard to reconcile the man with his sensitive poetry.

Augustus John was a complete contrast. Then in his sixties, he was a much more imposing figure. Tall and broad and with an impressive dark beard, John had been appointed as war artist to the Canadians and although as an officer beards were not permitted, he and King George V were the only two Army officers allowed to keep their facial decoration. When I first met him, with the Welsh poet, it was obvious they both drank to excess and this would lead to the early death of Dylan at thirty-eight-years-old.

It was Augustus John who introduced Dylan's future wife Caitlin to him, having himself reputedly once been her lover. This was a toxic world for someone like me, having been brought up with a strong Baptist influence. The conversation became more animated as they became more intoxicated.

I have to add that both these famous men did their best to chat us up when we were honoured by their company. Since my love was poetry rather than art, I was more interested in meeting Dylan and have continued to enjoy his poetry, especially his own reading of *Under Milk Wood* in the part of the narrator, since I have a much treasured and rare Caedmon copy of his BBC recording. At this time, however, I was very young and felt overwhelmed in the company of these two famous figures and would just stand and listen to their conversation. I think most of us who accompanied Zoe felt the same way.

Quentin F. Baillie – An Unrecorded Hero

I met Quentin by chance on Paddington Station. I was struggling with my baggage and he kindly helped me off the train. He was a Sergeant in the Royal Army Service Corps at the time. As I was waiting for a connection, I popped into the station café and he joined me. He told me he was stationed on the outskirts of London. In our short time together I learned a lot about him. He was a keen reader, he loved to travel and aimed after the war to work his way around the world.

By this time, I was no longer engaged and getting over the shock of losing George. Quentin was another Scot, lean and athletic and again with a Scottish brogue. I remember noting how well polished his boots were and the brilliant shine on his buttons. He later presented me with a button stick, to prevent the polish soiling my uniform.

We arranged to meet on a future occasion. Quentin was not particularly good looking but was a great companion with an enquiring mind. As we got to know each other better, he would often pop in to see my parents when in London and became a particular favourite with my mother. We established a firm friendship and I even discussed joining him on his world trek if we survived the war. Then he was posted abroad. He hinted to me that he had been transferred to Special Operations.

One day a parcel arrived for me – censored and packed in a tarred paper, marked Army Post Office. Inside was a book entitled *Mein Schitzenbuch*. It contained war sketches by a well-known German artist of scenes from the battle front. The pictures were so realistic, you felt right there. There were sketches of tank battles, a prisoner-of-war camp with portraits of prisoners and scenes of ravaged towns. The letter which accompanied it said Quentin had found it on the body of a German soldier. I often wonder about the owner, was he a Nazi or just an ordinary man who loved art. And had Quentin killed him?

This letter became one to treasure. Once more it was the last I would receive from someone I had come to love. Two months later my mother telephoned to say she had received a letter from Quentin. Her voice faltered when she read his words aloud, 'Dear friend, I want you to tell Eileen I will never see her again. I am too fond of her to inflict my problems on her.'

I wondered what was coming next but from the tone of my mother's voice, I knew it would be bad. He had been sent on a special mission, an attempted landing somewhere unknown. In the action, he had been badly injured and, he said, so crippled he would only be a burden to me. I was devastated. Once more someone very special had been taken away. Ever since, I have tried to find out what happened. I had no home address for him. I only knew he came from Dundee. I have checked with Army records but they will reveal nothing as I am not direct family. I still wonder what really happened.

Captain Jimmy Younghusband and the Stanmore Riding School

By May 1944, it was obvious British and American forces were planning a landing in France. The roads were full of army vehicles and equipment being moved. We had already been moved from the underground bunker at Bentley Priory as our Filter Room was designated to house the meetings of top-ranking officers from all the services, together with the Prime Minister, for planning sessions on the imminent invasion of Europe. We were now working above ground in a property commandeered by the RAF. A new Filter Room had been constructed in the spacious grounds of Hill House, opposite Stanmore Common and the Stanmore Riding School.

Orders came that all watches were to put on an event to encourage the civilian public to 'Save For Victory' – a national saving scheme to help the war effort. B watch decided we would run a garden party in the grounds of Hill House. The government had launched an appeal for the populace to invest in savings bonds. 'Wings for Victory' was the slogan. Fighter Command asked both the Filter and Ops Room watches to run an event to support this campaign. There would be a prize of National Savings Certificates for the watch raising the most money. My watch delegated me as organiser.

The team enrolled the support of local shops and businesses who donated prizes. We thought up many devices to extract money from the public – a treasure hunt, a fortune teller and hoopla, quoits and darts competitions – but since the participants would receive back in savings stamps any money they spent, the whole event would cost them nothing. Then I came up with the idea of pony rides for the children. I thought perhaps the riding school might loan us a couple of ponies. I walked across to the stables and met the owner, Captain Jimmy Younghusband. He was in his mid-fifties I guessed and had an air of command. Dressed in highly polished riding boots and leather breeches and holding a whip in his hand, he certainly looked the part.

I explained what we were planning and asked for his help. Could he let us have two of his ponies and a groom so we could offer rides for the children? Having served in the First World War in the Cavalry and being highly patriotic, he was delighted to cooperate.

The Captain, as he was known to all, had always been crazy about horses. Growing up in Chichester, his father was an impecunious curate but Jimmy offered his services for nothing in the local stables and proved to be a hard worker. The owner, Harry Field, took a fancy to him and taught him to ride. He was a natural horseman. However, things changed when his father died in his early thirties. Their mother, left with three boys, could not cope. The eldest son, Geoffrey, managed to obtain a bursary to university. The second, Cyril, was given £5 and sent off to Kenya to work on a farm and Jimmy was also given £5 and a free passage to Canada. He made his way across the Rockies and arrived in British Columbia in the far west, then a wild land still populated by the native Indians. He found work on a ranch and proved his worth with his horsemanship. He was young, strong and adaptable. He prospered and, with a partner, purchased some land and set up his own ranch.

Aged twenty-two at the outbreak of the First World War, he volunteered and returned home to join the Inniskilling Dragoon Guards. He was awarded the Military Cross. A handsome young man, he soon met and married Barbara Newman, known as Tommy, one of the Army nurses. She came from a Catholic family, distantly related to Cardinal Newman. Her father was a member of the Diplomatic Corps, having served in Queen Victoria's reign as Consul in Puerto Rico and also Siam. He later became a Queen's Messenger, charged with the delivery of secret documents. On his death, his daughter inherited his estate. This enabled the newlyweds to purchase the house and stables at Stanmore and establish the Stanmore Riding School.

This establishment soon became renowned, teaching many famous people to ride, including the young Elizabeth Taylor for her role in the film *National Velvet,* as well Janette Scott and Terence Stamp. It was rated as one of the top two riding establishments in the country. Captain Younghusband was one of the three founders of the Pony Club, the training ground for so many young riders even today.

Peter Younghusband – My Future Husband

The day of the Garden Party arrived, we had beautiful weather and the people came in their hordes to support us since there was little other entertainment on offer at the time. We succeeded in raising a large sum for the Wings for Victory campaign. The following day, I went over to the stables to thank the Captain for his help and was introduced to his wife.

Pleased with our success, Jimmy, as I was now told to call him, suggested that perhaps I and any friends from the Mess might like to use the Spring Ponds in his grounds for a swim. On this occasion Peter, his elder son, was home on a day off. He too was in the Air Force, serving at RAF Northolt nearby. He told me that he ran the station dance orchestra and if we ever ran a party or dance at our Mess, he and the orchestra would be pleased to come and play. And that was where our romance began.

A few days later, I decided to have a swim in the Spring Ponds. Peter happened to have a day off and we met again. He was very amusing and also good-looking. Like many of the RAF boys then, he wore a moustache, not a large bristly one but a smart well-trimmed one. We chatted away as if we had known each other for years. He was medium height and since I was only 5ft. 2 inches that suited me. I told him we would book the band for our next party in the Mess and we decided to meet for a swim again. Our friendship grew into something more on those grassy slopes by the waters of the Spring Ponds.

I learned he had always wanted to fly and had grown up with the two boys from the de Havilland family, the famous aircraft manufacturers. They arranged for him to have free flights at Hendon in their father's planes in exchange for riding lessons. Peter volunteered right at the beginning of the war for aircrew. He was sent to train as a Wireless Operator/Air Gunner.

Initially there were large numbers of applicants for aircrew for a limited number of available aircraft. To control the numbers for the aircraft available, all applicants had to fulfil every individual test. Peter got through all but one with flying colours but failed on his Morse. To his great disappointment, he was sent instead to train as a Physical Training Instructor. Before the war, he had been a drummer in a semi-pro dance band as a hobby and he was soon leader of the RAF Northolt station dance orchestra. Perhaps if he had been a wireless operator air gunner, he may not have survived since it was the 'WOP Aggies' who suffered the highest mortality rate.

I met Peter in May and by my birthday in July, we were engaged. I was welcomed into the family and was invited to spend my time, when off watch, at his home. I managed to see Peter occasionally when I was off-duty, since his home was close to where I worked at Stanmore and also he was stationed fairly close at RAF Northolt. In those times of uncertainty we all lived for the day, never knowing what was ahead. Peter and I set our wedding date for September 30th.

Despite rationing, we managed with help from friends to put on a reception for sixty guests, with a wedding cake made by the Fighter Command chef. We were loaned a hall in Edgware for the occasion as a wedding present. Elaine, a Filterer working with me on C-watch, made a beautiful dress, with material provided by donated clothing coupons. The guests were a mixture of my family, my fellow Officers, the staff of the riding school and some of the distinguished riding school clients, among them a galaxy of well-known people who I would meet many times afterwards as they joined the famous 'Sunday Ride' at the Stanmore Riding School. These were mostly older men such as Sir Frederick Handley Page, the aircraft tycoon, Sir Harry Hague who was the owner of the company producing Ovaltine, and Gus Neill of Bravingtons the jewellers. It was through him that Peter obtained my engagement ring with my favourite stone, an opal, and the wedding ring of 22-carat gold even though the regulations said only 9-carat gold should be used. Peter had grown up with these people. I found them rather intimidating at first but they gave me a great welcome. Despite rationing, the gifts we received were beautiful – often antiques from their own collections.

Bill Hooper, the RAF cartoonist, was our best man and our bridesmaid was a young Belgian girl who had just escaped from her country before the Germans invaded. We went on a three-day honeymoon to Rottingdean. Five weeks later, we would be separated.

Bill Hooper – The Cartoonist RAFF

Bill Hooper, a buddy of Peter's, was very happy to be our best man. Ex-aircrew, he sported an enormous moustache with an air of bravado. He was well-known throughout the RAF for his famous character Pilot Officer Prune. Bill looked rather like his drawings of this amiable but gormless pilot.

P.O. Prune appeared in all Bill's cartoons – he was the pilot who always did the wrong thing and was used as a salutary lesson to aircrew to look and learn. Many of his famous cartoons decorated the walls of the Abercorn Arms on Stanmore Hill, the pub where Fighter Command aircrew often congregated. The cartoon I particularly remember was a scene under the sea – P.O. Prune looking very bewildered with fish swimming round the aircraft and sea weed waving around the cockpit. The caption was 'When P.O. Prune failed to pull out of his dive in time!'

Bill joined the Air Force at the start of the war and trained as an air gunner but later transferred to ground staff where he met Anthony Armstrong, editor of the RAF training manual 'Tee Emm'. Together they created the character of P.O. Prune as a way of instructing wartime pilots of what not to do if they wanted to save their lives and their aircraft.

After the war Bill created a number of successful books and became the political cartoonist for the *Sunday Chronicle*. Later he was the presenter of 'Willy the Pup' for the BBC. He also produced a strip cartoon for the *Star* newspaper before returning to television as an artist and later a presenter. Unsurprisingly, our wedding present was a cartoon.

Ignace Kennis and Life in Belgium

Five weeks after our wedding, I received the news that I was to be posted overseas. I was being sent to 2nd Tactical Air Force at Malines (now Mechelen) in recently liberated Belgium for a secret task. Peter could not believe it and asked me why, as a married woman, I had been chosen since this was normally not allowed. I could not tell him any details of my work as I had signed the Official Secrets Act and was unable to discuss my role for thirty years after war ended. In fact neither he nor my son ever knew what my work as a Filterer Officer entailed or what I did in Belgium.

Arriving in Malines, I found I would be sharing an Officers' Mess with predominantly male RAF and Royal Services Corps officers. The eight WAAF Filters selected were given the task of finding the launch sites of the V2 rockets targeting Antwerp. This was our first usable port and it was being bombarded daily by V2s. By now, the Allies had the Germans in retreat. Unable to use their static launch sites, they had now resorted to mobile launching from lorries with trailers. Moving away from their bases, they would choose different sites daily, sometimes at the coast, sometimes in woodland or even town car parks, for these deadly weapons.

The Mess building we were to occupy had previously been the *Soldatenheim* where the German troops had been billeted. We, however, had to sleep in billets in the town. The house I was sent to was the home of Ignace Kennis, a famous Belgian artist. He and his wife did not take kindly to providing accommodation for a foreign woman and during all the time I was there, we barely exchanged more than a few words.

The room I was allocated was dark with heavy velvet curtains. On the walls were religious paintings, painted by Kennis himself I imagined. An enormous cross hung above the bed which I constantly expected to fall on me! The room always smelt musty. He and his wife were probably only in their fifties but they looked much older. They spoke Flemish among themselves and heavily accented French if they deigned to speak to me. I never felt at home there. My bedroom, the sole area other than the bathroom I was allowed to use, was devoid of any comforts – an enormous ancient wooden bed and a wardrobe, not even a chair so I spent as little time as possible there.

The artist himself was a small shrunken man, dour and slightly grubby and his wife even more unattractive and unwelcoming. I realised that like their fellow countrymen, they had suffered from the German-occupying army and were suspicious of any other occupying army, even though we had come to free them. Food was still short. They had had to rummage in the dustbins of the German soldiers for scraps of food. This continued even after we arrived. My memories of my host were hardly happy ones. Later I would learn how respected he was as a painter.

Three Belgian Pierres

The town of Malines had a very active hockey club, most of the members also being in the Belgian national ice hockey team. They offered us the hospitality of their club house. It was there that I met the handsome Conrad brothers, Pierre and Theo. They were both about the same age as I was and we soon became great friends. I would frequently be invited to their home which was close to our base. They, and especially Pierre, would help me to overcome my sudden departure from my new husband after such a brief few weeks.

Pierre's family owned a prosperous timber company with sawmills in the Ardennes forest. Soon after our arrival in Belgium, the von Rundstedt Offensive, also known as the Battle of the Bulge, was launched. General von Rundstedt's troops were deployed in the Ardennes to try and cut off the American force in the south from the British forces which were now heading towards Rotterdam. It was a crucial time for us in Malines. We would have been captured if they had managed to reach their target city of Antwerp, only 10 kilometres from us. By late January 1945, the Allies had successfully defeated the onslaught.

Pierre was anxious to know whether his workmen at his sawmill in the Ardennes were safe and whether there had been much damage to his sawmill. He asked me if I would like to go with him. I jumped at the chance to see more of Belgium and perhaps cross the border into France and I readily agreed. In early February, at the first opportunity of a day off-duty, we set off in one of the company lorries since Pierre decided to pick up some timber at the same time.

It had been a harsh winter, contributing to the difficulties in the conflict. A fierce battle had been fought between the German Panzers and the USA tank regiments supported by a smaller contingent of British. Hundreds of men were killed on both sides and many tanks destroyed. The snow had covered the bodies.

By the time we set out, the snow was beginning to melt. To our horror, as we drove through the forest, we saw the emerging corpses of the victims – German, American and British together amidst the damaged tanks. It was a horrific sight, the bodies lay where they had fallen. We were shocked; neither of us could speak, mentally reliving what had occurred so recently. We continued our journey in silence until we reached Bastogne, the town that had been the site of a particularly violent battle. We found a café open amidst the ruins and sat down quietly, trying to get over the horrors we had seen and realising that if the outcome had been different, Mechelen and its inhabitants would have fallen to the enemy. For Pierre, there had been one bright spot in the day – all his workmen had survived and his sawmill was intact. For me, it was a journey I would never forget.

In 1935, I had met two Belgian youngsters, Pierre and Yvette Serruys at a roller-skating rink in Middelkerke while on holiday there. We were friends for a week and continued to keep in occasional touch by letter before the war. On a rare day off, I managed to trace their address in Brussels. I called on the off-chance they were still there. They recognised me immediately and made me welcome. This would be a family I would visit frequently, usually taking a packet of coffee beans for them. I learnt how their mother had been heavily involved in the Resistance movement and Pierre with her. They were part of a team helping Allied pilots who had baled out of aircraft or escaped from captivity to get to a neutral county and eventually return to Britain. They had a cellar in their house where the pilots would be hidden until they were passed on to the next phase of their escape. Often empty wine barrels would be used, hiding the pilots inside them, and then they would be rolled along the route to the next safe house. During the occupation Pierre and his mother were risking their lives daily.

The third Pierre, Pierre Lizon, I had met with his family during a rare visit home on leave. The family had just escaped on the last boat to leave Antwerp before the Germans engulfed their country. Translating their French, I was able to help them tell their story at the local police station where they went to register and obtain advice. I kept in touch with them and their daughter was my bridesmaid. When they heard I was going to Belgium after its liberation, they gave me contacts with their family members who lived in Grimbergen, a suburb of Brussels. They would send me parcels of coffee beans, still obtainable in Britain. In Belgium, there had been no coffee since war began, instead acorns were being ground up as a poor substitute – I was a very popular visitor.

Paris and Marcel Boucher's Fall From Grace

Our operation had suffered a setback in the late December. The weather was so bad that the Mosquitos were unable to fly. Consequently the number of V2s launched had temporarily increased. However, by late February the weather had improved and we had managed to destroy most of the launch lorries; they were not being replaced in time by the manufacturers and the Allied forces were advancing closer to the German launch sites. There was little for us to do so we were given additional duties.

I was detailed to go to the Supreme Headquarters of the Allied Expeditionary Force (SHAEF) in Paris, based at the Palace of Versailles to report on progress of Operation Strongbow, the codename for our operation against the V2s. While there, I thought I would try to find out what had happened to Marcel Boucher and his family after I had been forced so unexpectedly to leave them as an au pair.

I knew they owned a hotel in Paris – Hôtel de la Trémoille – and on my first free afternoon, I made my way there. I found the American army had taken it over. The officer in charge initially greeted me courteously and asked me what I wanted. I explained I had worked for the owners of the hotel just before the war and was anxious to know they were safe. His attitude changed immediately and he became very officious. He asked to see my papers and refused to give me any information about them. I was anxious by now and persisted, saying, 'You must know something!'

Eventually he said, 'I cannot give you any more information – you must forget about them.' This not only surprised me but made me think. If they had been killed, he surely would have told me, so what could have happened?

Thirty-five years later I learned the truth. After the German occupation this much-respected Deputé had joined the Vichy government, under Marshal Pétain, in the then-unoccupied south of France, although his family returned to their hotel in Paris. By 1944, he recognised that the Germans were losing the war and he escaped with his family to Germany. Some time later, getting permission from the Vatican, he entered Italy, and a few months afterwards, crossed into Spain to Barcelona. From there the family took a ship to Rio de Janeiro and like many renegade collaborators, started a new life in the Argentine.

During General de Gaulle's presidency, Marcel Boucher was charged as a pétainist – considered a collaborator and all his possessions confiscated. Since his wife was the legal owner of the hotel, she was allowed to retain possession of it although she too had left France.

It was not until 1990 that I learned the rest of the story. In 1950, at the time of the presidency of Vincent Auriol, Boucher had returned to France to plead his innocence. He had been trained as a lawyer and put forward a convincing plea that he was never pro-Hitler but always anti-communism and the Popular Front.

He was most eloquent and they believed him and restored his possessions. He immediately sold everything and left France, returning to Argentina. He eventually died in 1968 during a visit to his dentist in Montevideo, Uruguay. But I recall his close friendship with the Romanian Prime Minister who had expressed strong anti-Semitic views. I doubt the truth of his plea especially since he was part of the Pétain government, considered a collaboration party. Amazingly, only a few months ago a French author I met, Geneviève Moulard, managed to trace the little girl, Hélène, now seventy-nine-years-old. After an adventurous life, she was living in Geneva. We now regularly converse by telephone.

Roger Sirdey

Whilst in Paris, I decided to find my brother's pen pal, Roger Sirdey. I traced him to a Paris suburb where he lived with his parents. He was four years younger than me and quite shy and, although he had studied English, loath to speak it.

He too had been involved in the Resistance. Leaving school, although very clever, he was unable to go to university because of the occupation. He found a job as a delivery boy for an ironmonger. The owner of the business was the leader of a local Resistance cell and was obtaining information of German troop movements through a connection with an army garrison close by.

Learning that Roger spoke passable German, the leader enrolled him into the cell and he was given the job of delivering any items ordered by the German troops, stationed nearby. He was instructed to get friendly with them, talk to them in their own language and to keep his eyes and ears peeled for information about troop movements and to report arrivals of important people to the camp.

He managed to make friends with the guards and surreptitiously acquired a lot of useful information for the Resistance. However, on the day peace was declared, the French populace was singling out people suspected of being Nazi sympathisers. People living and working close to the ironmonger's shop could not have failed to notice how friendly Roger had been with the German soldiers and, having no knowledge of the shop owner's Resistance work, they were waiting for him the following morning as he arrived on his bike for work. They started beating him up. His employer rushed out and after a lot of effort, managed to convince the mob that both he and Roger were members of the Resistance – but not before Roger suffered some injury. I am still in touch with him and have visited him in Perpignan where he now lives in retirement after a successful career as manager of a thriving cement company. He will never talk about his wartime activities; he says there are too many painful memories.

Paul le Rumeur and the French Connection

Through the twinning of the towns of Penarth in South Wales and St-Pol-de-Léon in Brittany, I became great friends with another Frenchman who had sad memories of the war. Paul le Rumeur was a well-known local dentist in St Pol and a great anglophile. During a conversation about how the German occupation had affected his family, I learnt the sad story of his brother.

The two boys were brought up in the city of Morlaix. The German troops had gained a bad reputation in the city, committing many brutal acts and raping the women. The feeling against them grew very strong and eventually the Resistance killed several of the German soldiers. The local Commander of the German Army planned his revenge. The following Saturday night when the young people were out on the town enjoying themselves, the German troops captured twenty-five young men and announced they were to be imprisoned as a warning against any further anti-German acts.

Paul's brother was one of these young men. The family did not know for a long time that these French captives had been incarcerated in a camp in the Harz Mountains, together with many Russian soldiers from the Eastern Front. They were put to work to build the V2 rockets, after the original site at Peenemünde had been bombed. They worked long hours, food was scarce and much of what was available was stolen from the weaker prisoners by the Russians. It would not be until many years later that he learned how his brother had died – he had starved to death.

Two Escaped Prisoners of War and VE Day

It was May 8th, we knew victory was imminent as all enemy air activity had ceased but we were still manning our stations. At 0800 hours on that morning in 1945 I came off duty and walked over towards the Mess, ready for breakfast. Suddenly a small black car with German number plates jerked to a halt in front of me. Out jumped two British pilots who rushed towards me. They hugged me and one started to cry. 'You are the first English woman we have seen since 1940,' his companion said. It was then I noticed on the side of their car a scrawled PWX. They were ex-prisoners of war – both bomber pilots, shot down in their Wellington at the beginning of air operations in 1940 and imprisoned in a camp north of Hanover.

Four days earlier, it had become obvious to the inmates that something unusual was happening; the prison guards had started deserting their posts and disappearing. Rumours ran around the camp that the war was nearly over in Germany. The two pilots seized the opportunity to steal one of the S.S. guards' cars when it was dark. They travelled through Germany at night and even kept under the cover of darkness when they reached Holland, since they were not sure if the war was yet over. When short of petrol, they filched it from farm tractors and they laid low during daylight hours. As they entered Belgium, they realised that they were finally in liberated territory and I was the first obviously British person they had seen since their escape.

On hearing their story, I was overcome with emotion. I took them over to the Mess and made sure they had a super breakfast since they had been surviving on fruit from the wayside and roots from the fields together with what little they had secreted from their rations before leaving the camp. By 11 o'clock the news had come that Germany had announced unconditional surrender and the war in Europe was over. Although we had been expecting it, the news caused great joy and celebration in the Mess.

The Commanding Officer asked the two pilots what they wanted to do and they said without a thought that they wanted to go back to Rotterdam and find the nurses who had saved their lives after the crash. They particularly wanted to take food to them, knowing the terrible shortage in Holland. The C.O. told me to get the cooks to prepare a large box of food – tins of meat and vegetables, eggs, cheese and biscuits – and he ordered me to take another WAAF officer with me and stay with them throughout the journey. He was worried that they might become 'bomb-happy', an expression used when aircrew got over-excited and perhaps had a mishap during an operation.

About midday we set off on our journey to Rotterdam. As we passed through the towns and villages, we met cheering crowds and processions of farm carts and wagons, piled high with branches of broom from the hedges, aglow with their glorious golden flowers – a tribute to the much-loved rulers of the country, the House of Orange. It was a journey to be remembered forever.

But on arriving at the banks of the River Rhine, we were devastated to find that the bridge leading to the city of Rotterdam had been blown up by the retreating Germans. Searching for a means to cross by boat, we found a ferryman arriving in a flat-bottomed boat, loaded with supplies for the villagers. We asked if he would ferry us across – we pleaded with him but he refused and for a good reason. The river was full of mines. Alone with just a light cargo of food, he could manage to cross safely but with even one of us and the large box of food we had with us, the boat would be much lower in the water. There would be little chance of missing one of the deadly weapons. Reluctantly, we had to unload the food and ask him to take it to the hospital. We gave him the address and the names of the nurses and just hoped they would receive their much deserved thank you present. I knew how valuable food was on the black market and could not help but suspect that it would never reach its intended destination.

All four of us piled back in the S.S. car and headed to Brussels. There we were welcomed by rapturous crowds who greeted us with cheers as we paraded with the rest of the Allied cars, through the streets to the Grande Place. The people of Brussels lined the streets, dressed in their best and delirious with joy and relief. They showered us with bouquets of flowers and cakes made especially for the celebration. They ransacked their cellars for treasured bottles of wine and offered us glasses along the route. The two pilots, ecstatic at realising they were free and their ordeal over, were sobbing one moment with relief and then laughing with joy the next. How glad I was not to have missed it.

The Collaborators and Belgian Members of the S.S. at Breendonk

There are some men I would never have chosen to meet. In May 1945, as soon as the peace treaty was signed, I was ordered to undertake a task which in my wildest nightmares I could never have imagined.

I was driven daily to the district of Willebroek, north of Brussels, to act as guide and interpreter in the fortress at Breendonk, known as the Camp of Silence and of Death. Built prior to World War One, it was briefly used in the Second World War as the General Headquarters of King Leopold III, in charge of the Belgian armed forces. It fell to the enemy after only a seven-day siege. After its surrender, it was transformed into a concentration camp, initially used as a transit camp for Jewish prisoners en route to Auschwitz.

After the arrival of Kommandant Schmitt, a crueller and more rigorous regime was instituted, resulting in the death of many before they could be sent on to Auschwitz. It has now been recognised that despite being only a small facility, it was one of the cruellest in its treatment. It gained a grim reputation as a place of torture and interrogation of a wide variety of prisoners, including resistance fighters, communists, homosexuals and gypsies. Of the 3,500 incarcerated there, 1,733 did not survive the war, three hundred were killed in the camp and in addition, almost one hundred succumbed to either starvation or torture.

Over a period of three weeks, I was detailed to act as guide and interpreter to groups of RAF personnel I showed daily around this camp. I took them to the punishment cells, the torture chamber and pointed out the inscriptions on the walls, scratched into the surface by the broken nails of the prisoners, recording their days and weeks of imprisonment. Some who had suffered in these cells had recorded the names of those who had betrayed them. One had written, '*Betraihi par ma maitresse, Leonardine Boissons de Courtrai*'– betrayed by my mistress, Leonardine Boissons of Courtrai.

I showed them the bloodied posts of where those destined to be executed were tied. This difficult assignment was intended to ensure the British airmen would learn what had happened under the Nazis; the torture and the inhuman treatment inflicted on the prisoners.

By the time I arrived, the few surviving prisoners had been freed and it now housed Belgian citizens accused of being traitors and spies. The majority were young men who had joined the Belgian S.S., committing atrocities quite as horrible as those of the Germans serving there. These men were usually exercising in the courtyard as I crossed through. After a few days, they must have learned what I was doing and took every opportunity to harass me. If out of sight of their guards, they would urinate at me and yell obscenities. I very soon became hardened and would walk through to the main entrance, holding my head high and ignoring them. But many times since I have relived those moments, remembering when I met the scum of humanity. At night I wake up and visualise again the torture chamber and see the tragic inscriptions on the cell walls.

Group Captain Bajn and his Colleagues

On my return home to Fighter Command Headquarters, I learnt details of my next mission; it would be one that was a mixture of pleasure and pain. I was given the task of improving the ability to speak and write correct English to a group of senior Polish fighter pilots. They were all much older than I was but treated me with great respect. Group Captain Bajn was the most senior. He had served in the First World War as a pilot in the Polish Air Force, where he had lost a hand in battle. He now had a prosthesis and always wore a glove. The others were either Squadron Leaders or Flight Lieutenants, all with a record of many 'kills' to their names.

The pain came from the fact that Russia had now taken over Poland and these men were unable to return home and join their families. The pleasure was being able to help them to establish themselves in Britain. Initially their speech was heavily accented and peppered with RAF slang

– pukka job, wizard prang and so on – probably indecipherable to most of the civilian population. I based my lessons on all the sounds included in the use of Pitman's shorthand! They were a delightful bunch of men, attractive, eager to learn, willing to study hard and trying their hardest to face the fact they might never see their families again. They were so polite and grateful for my help and applied themselves to learn all they could.

Finally after working with them for over six months, they were demobilised. After their last lesson, they presented me with a book entitled *Poland's Progress* signed with all their exotic names. I have never heard from any of them since and wonder whether they managed to become British and if their families have been able to join them but occasionally I pick up that book and think of them and hope they are happy.

Civilian Again

The Film Star Set and the Dance Band Connection

By 1946, the film studios were coming back to life and Jimmy Younghusband and his horses were involved in many of the films of the day. Often there were riding scenes and many of the stars had to be taught the elementary means of staying on a horse and not falling off.

The veteran actor A.E. Matthews lived nearby in Bushey Heath and had appeared in many films where Jimmy Younghusband had provided the horses. He was a familiar figure in the stable yard, where he would chat with the stable girls and pat the horses on the nose. Whenever we met, I would delight in hearing his voice which despite his age – he was by then in his seventies – would be as strong and rich as a young man's.

The same year Jimmy provided the horses for the musical drama film *The Laughing Lady* and one of the leading actors learning to ride was Webster Booth. He and Anne Ziegler were frequent visitors to the riding school and regulars on the Sunday ride. The first outing my son had, after returning from the nursing home, was to be pushed by them in his pram down to the local pub where all the riders congregated before lunch. Another frequent visitor was Terence Stamp, then a young hopeful making his way as an extra. With so many film studios in the area, there was always someone learning the rudiments of equestrian skills at the stables. Sadly I never had the opportunity to meet George Arliss, who appeared in *The House of Rothschild*, when my father-in-law took his place in all the riding scenes.

Vernon Herbert

Immediately after being demobbed, Peter's semi-pro dance orchestra was getting many bookings and frequently played at the Victoria Halls in Southampton Row. We both became close friends with the general manager of the resident caterers, Vernon Herbert. He was about ten years older than Peter and had many interesting connections in the culinary world. He was a handsome man, tall and very distinguished with a greying goatee beard. At the time, rationing was still de rigueur and no restaurant could charge more for a meal than five shillings, so you can imagine how difficult this was for the top London restaurants to cope. They could only recoup their profit with restricted choices and augment the charges for wines and other beverages.

On one occasion Vernon invited us to dine with him at the Trocadero. He was friends with both the manager and the maitre chef so we had a very un-rationed meal. We were each given an enormous printed menu in a large leather cover to choose from and then instructed to stand them up in front of our plates so nobody could check what we were eating! He and his then wife became frequent visitors later when we moved to the West Country Inn in Hartland. In many ways he would affect our future lives.

Sir Colin Cole and the Territorial Regiments at Camp

In 1948, out of the blue, came an invitation from Peter's cousin for us to change direction and become hoteliers running her hotel in north Devon as she intended buying a second one in Wincanton. Ever ready for a challenge, we upped sticks and took over the West Country Inn, 'the last Inn in Devon', situated on a lonely coastal road on Bursdon Moor. Three miles from the village of Hartland, ten miles from Bude and fifteen miles from Bideford, possible customers seemed few and far between. Petrol continued to be rationed until 1953. Initially we relied on the local farmers and their workers and a very occasional commercial traveller who would have official red petrol for work purposes. However, we started to specialise in gourmet meals and gradually built up a reputation. I cooked, Peter waited tables and a local girl did the housework.

Our clientele grew, our fame increased and one day a bevy of Army officers booked in for lunch. They came from Cleave Camp, just outside Bude. From April until October, the camp had Territorial Regiments training there from the Royal Artillery. The first visitors enjoyed their meal and booked a date for their final Regimental dinner at the end of camp. This was the 523 (Gloucester) Light Ack Ack Regiment and they came every year from then on – the following year I created a special dessert named after them. They enjoyed themselves sufficiently to leave our phone number and a hearty recommendation on the wall of the telephone box in the Officers' Mess.

From then on, most of the regiments used us for their own celebrations and this led to us meeting, and in some case establishing long friendships with, interesting officers who led important lives as civilians. One of the most celebrated was Sir Colin Cole. After his wartime service with the Coldstream Guards, he originally trained for a legal career but in 1953, he migrated to the College of Arms as Fitzalan Pursuivant of Arms Extraordinary and by 1978 he was named Garter Principal King of Arms. We kept in touch in the following years and in the 1980s, he was instrumental in creating the coat of arms of a close friend of mine, Christopher Pollard, when he was elected High Sheriff for the Welsh county of South Glamorgan.

During one of Sir Colin's visits to Wales, I joined him at the final of the rugby match between England and Wales. We were in the VIP boxes and the only two in the vicinity shouting for England!

Sir Edward Heath

The future Prime Minister, Lieut. Colonel Edward Heath came annually to our hotel with his regiment, the famous Honourable Artillery

Company. This regiment of pike men and musketeers was formed in the era of Charles I and renowned for having permission to parade through the London streets with their ornate pikes held aloft.

Whenever Edward Heath arrived for the annual regimental dinner, it was pretty obvious he had no desire to talk to a woman and never seemed to join in the bonhomie of his fellow officers. He was a stolid type, not at all forthcoming. I only ever saw him in uniform which was always impeccable but he never seemed to smile, even when the rest of his colleagues were enjoying themselves. I would try to avoid him since he looked at me with such disdain whenever we were in contact. I would never have believed that he would head a future government of the United Kingdom.

Robert Henriques

Another of the colonels visiting the West Country Inn each year was the author Robert Henriques, also a 'Terrier', and a member of one of the oldest Jewish families in Britain. A man of many parts, he was a farmer, writer and broadcaster and had gained renown for two award-winning novels and biographies of Jewish tycoons. He had joined the Territorial Army before the war, serving first in the Royal Artillery and later with Combined Operations. Post-war he returned to the Territorials. A man of great charm, even as an Army Officer, he still had the weathered look of a farmer and seemed as happy talking about his animals with Peter, as talking with army pals. His book *No Arms, No Armour* (1939) came out to considerable critical praise. In 1943 Henriques published *Captain Smith and Company* which drew upon his wartime experience. It tells the stories of 'Captain Smith' and other members of his company of Commandos. They were elite army units created by Winston Churchill's direct order after Dunkirk as a means of raiding and harassing German forces on Continental Europe. The novel recounts how different men in Captain Smith's company were recruited, or felt compelled to enlist, while revealing diverse aspects of their civilian backgrounds. One of them is a poet. Apart from these flashback episodes, the novel describes the training of the men and their active service raiding a coastal facility in Norway, setting explosive charges to blow up a bridge and then, when the bridge is destroyed, the reflections and slow lingering deaths of Smith and other comrades. I am sure a lot of these episodes were based on his experiences.

Peter, Lord Moynihan

Peter, Lord Moynihan was another regular Territorial visitor and was always most courteous to me, which was not always the case with some of the more junior Territorial officers. Trained as a barrister, he became a stockbroker. As a member of the House of Lords, he took the Liberal Whip. I was surprised to read that in April 1965, he was charged with 'persistently importuning for an immoral purpose'. He was taken ill and died just a few days before he was due to appear at Bow Street Magistrates' Court. I had seen no signs of this frailty and he often talked to me about his wife and family. It made me realise that one can never truly know anyone.

Ronald Duncan

Ronald Duncan, the author, journalist and poet was another frequent and most interesting customer who farmed locally. He was born with the name Dunkelsbühler in Salisbury, Rhodesia, now Zimbabwe, and was, I believe, of mixed ancestry. He was a swarthy man – very slight and with masses of hair. He was never still; his eyes constantly darting from one corner to the next.

He is best remembered for his play *This Way to the Tomb* and as the librettist for *The Rape of Lucretia*, an opera which he co-wrote with Benjamin Britten. However, during the time I knew him, he was contributing to the *London Evening News* a column about life in Devon, entitled 'Jan Stewer's Diary', an amusing account of daily happenings on his farm and in the local village of Welcombe.

He was renowned as an ardent pacifist but my special remembrance of him was of the day he sent me an SOS by telephone, to say his wife Rosemary was away. He was in a panic because Henry Williamson, the author of *Tarka the Otter,* was coming to stay for a few days. During his wife's absence, the house had become more than a little untidy. He wanted to know if one of my staff in the hotel could come and clean the bath. As there was no one on duty at the time, I offered to do it myself. I had an ulterior motive – I hoped to meet the visiting author as I had always loved the book. I told Ronald my only condition was that I should be introduced to Mr Williamson.

Henry Williamson

The creator of Tarka was a quiet bespectacled man. It was obvious from the short conversation I had with him that he loved the countryside and field sports. He told me he hoped to take his gun out and get a few pheasants so I mentioned my husband was a keen shot and that, if he would pop in to the West Country Inn, Peter would be delighted to show him the best spots to stalk. He called at the hotel the next day and brought me back a pheasant after a successful afternoon's shooting. Sadly in later years he suffered from dementia and he died on the very day that filming of *Tarka the Otter* started.

Ewart Hodgson

One of our most frequent visitors from London was an old wartime friend of Peter's: Ewart Hodgson, an eloquent man with a wonderful command of words. He was the brilliant film critic for the *News of the World*.

In a review of Jane Russell, he coined the famous words, 'Mean... moody...magnificent'. Even today his classic review of the film *Canterbury Tales*, written, produced and directed by Michael Powell and

Emeric Pressburger appears on the internet.

He frequently stayed with us at the Inn and on one occasion he wrote in the visitors' book, 'Peace, good food and no Grable.' I still recall one of his more pithy sayings; he stood at an upstairs window, looking out to the empty ocean from the rocky north Devon coastline and he declaimed, 'Nothing but J. Arthur Rank going backwards and forwards!' It was true. We rarely saw any vessels on that vast expanse of water.

Bill Gifford

One of the 'locals' at the Inn who perhaps would not be considered memorable has remained in my memory as a link to the days when the north Devon coast was renowned for its wreckers in the seventeenth century. The Gifford family of that time were notorious for their activities luring passing ships into a supposed safe haven and then stealing the cargoes from the wrecks. Bill had the air of a buccaneer and was well-known to the local police. He would come in each evening for his regular tipple of a 'half and half' – half mild and half bitter beer – giving any visitor to the area a rendering of popular songs on his accordian and finally encouraging them to pay for the next round. His present occupation was a little more respectable than his forefathers' – he was a scrap-metal dealer and he was a delightful rogue.

Alfred Noyes – Show Biz at the Winter Gardens

In 1956 Peter's relatives decided to sell the West Country Inn and move to South Africa. It was time for a change. Through our old friend, Vernon Herbert, who had been a frequent guest at the Inn and had realised we had successfully mastered the art of catering, we were offered the management of the Winter Gardens at Ventnor on the Isle of Wight. This would entail organising regular entertainments – dances, conferences and concerts – as well as running the bars and a restaurant.

One of the first Winter Gardens was built in 1875 in the town centre of Blackpool, Lancashire. It included a theatre, ballroom and conference facilities. Many other towns adopted the name idea. Ventnor Urban District Council decided in 1929 to build their Winter Gardens on the site of the old parsonage, which was situated on the most coveted site in the south of the island with unsurpassed views out to sea. The new modern art deco building was designed to accommodate seven-hundred seated people and up to a thousand dancers on a beautiful dance floor. It was opened on the 17th August 1936.

It was the island's most modern-looking building. Painted cream with green window frames and a prominent glass-fronted staircase tower it quickly became a landmark from the sea approach. However by the late 1950s the type of entertainment it offered was no longer popular and several companies had become bankrupt trying to run it. Vernon Herbert's company, Nuthalls Caterers, decided to add it to their portfolio of seaside establishments. He offered us the job of running it, knowing Peter's dance-band connections.

We realised the new position would offer a huge challenge and we had to come up with new ideas. We decided to introduce a continental type of entertainment, free entry but serving drinks and food at the table for the audiences, offering a cabaret entertainment each night. This would range from talent nights to musical evenings with a small dance area set aside for the new swing. This was supplemented with a Saturday dance and a Sunday Palm Court concert. We hoped to encourage visitors to spend more than one evening with us. In addition to this, we became responsible for restoring the entertainment and catering on the town's pier once more. Early in the war, the centre of the structure had been removed in order to prevent possible landings by German troops. This had now been replaced and new facilities built.

Peter was in his element. We appointed a resident three-piece band, the Doug Carver Trio. They introduced us to the new sound of electronic guitars. Every Sunday we used local musicians for a Palm Court Orchestra and I would read, as a disembodied voice, a poem;

perhaps Masefield's 'Sea Fever' or even introduce a touch of Shakespeare.

One of the events we put on was a variety concert with local acts. One day we were short of items so I volunteered to do a recitation of 'The Highwayman' by Alfred Noyes. This poet had written many poems and books, at one time being judged as a pacifist, despite having served in the First World War. I had learned this narrative poem in my early teens and could recite it at a drop of a hat. On the night I appeared with appropriate dramatic lighting and declaimed it with gusto. I received what, I imagined, was polite applause from the audience.

When the show was over, I was approached by an elderly man in his mid-seventies. He was walking with a stick very slowly. He shook my hand before saying, 'I wrote that poem, you know!' It was Alfred Noyes himself. I asked him if he had enjoyed hearing it recited, and he said it was the first time he had had that experience and I had done justice to his words. I was over the moon.

In 1998, I made a return visit to the island to visit a cousin. I told him the story and was informed that Noyes' son, Hugh, was still living in his father's house. I telephoned him, saying that I had met his father once in the 1950s and explained the circumstances. He invited me for coffee and gave me a photocopy of the first draft of the poem. Some years later when doing a course with the Open University in Sociolinguistics, I used this document in one of my dissertations. Even now I sometimes have a go at seeing how much I can recall of that great narrative poem.

The wind was a torrent of darkness among the gusty trees,
The moon was a ghostly galleon tossed upon cloudy seas
The road was a ribbon of moonlight over the purple moor
And the highwayman came riding, riding, riding up to the old inn door.

Noyes' last poem, 'Ballade of the Breaking Shell', was written in May 1958, barely two years after our meeting and only one month before his death. He died at the age of seventy-seven, and is buried in the Roman Catholic cemetery at Freshwater on the island.

Duncan Simonds and Other Businessmen

Simonds Brewery had a great history. It was founded in 1785 and had provided beer for the army during many wars since then. Sadly in 1960 it was bought up by Courage and Company. In 1958 we became hoteliers again, employed by them. Our first appointment was to one of their houses in Reading. The assignment was to improve the image of a town pub with rooms.

The pub at the time was the haunt of local prostitutes and Irish labourers hired to build the local nuclear site at Aldermaston. To improve the image, we raised the prices, banned the prostitutes and opened a small lunchtime eatery, catering for the offices nearby. We lived in a couple of rooms above the bars. In those days, licensing hours meant we were closed in the afternoons.

One afternoon, fed up with the decor in the club meeting room, we decided to repaint it ourselves. We were interrupted by a knock on the door. It was an unexpected visit from the managing director, Duncan Simonds himself, come to check up on how we were getting on. He was an elegant man with a high forehead and beautiful hands and was most apologetic for calling during our supposed rest period. He was surprised to find us in overalls and clasping paint brushes. We explained what we were doing and he was so impressed that a week later, we were told we were being moved to Swindon to one of the brewery's prime hotels. From then onwards he kept a friendly eye on us.

The Goddard Arms, our new base, held many important functions. Five Masonic Lodges used its facilities monthly and the Rotary Club met there every week, so we came in contact with all the worthies of the town. Our time there coincided with a period of growth when Swindon was called an expanded London town, and many new industries moved their factories to the area. We would play host to personnel from companies such as Pressed Steel and Plessey. In addition, it played an important role in the railway network since the locomotive workshops were the greatest employer in the town.

Every day one or other of the well-known industrialists would be dining at our hotel. One of the first ones we met was H. V. Slade of Garrard Engineering, the pioneers of the very best of high-quality gramophone turntables. The company was a spin-off from Garrard and Co, the jewellers, and was formed in 1915 to create precision rangefinders. It was then sharing premises with the Plessey Company who would, during our tenure at Swindon, buy the company.

The Managing Director of the Plessey Company, Allen Clark, soon to be knighted, together with the local director, Teddy Underwood were regular customers. I became a friend to both of them and found myself being used as their public-relations link. Regularly they would ask me to join them when entertaining overseas clients as the coffee and liqueurs were being served.

There was a reason behind this request. Having imbibed rather a lot of alcohol, they realised they might forget what promises they had made or deals they had offered to the representatives of other large companies present. My brief was to listen to their conversation and remind them at breakfast the following morning what they had said!

Sir Allen was very popular with the hotel staff as he always left them very generous tips. He was especially kind to my son, then ten-years-old, bringing him a special fishing rod after a visit to the States. Teddy Underwood remained a friend for many years afterwards and I would see him whenever I went to London for committee meetings with Hotelympia in the years to come.

When any of the five Masonic Lodges had their monthly dinners at the hotel, my husband and I would personally run the bar out of courtesy to them (and also to ensure their contract) but of course when the signal was given 'The Lodge is tiled', we had to make a hasty departure. Little did they know I already knew all their secrets. For a short period after selling the West Country Inn, we ran a small pig and poultry farm near Barnstaple in the grounds of a big house. The owner, Major Malins, had rejoined the Army and had been posted overseas. He had asked us to keep an eye on his manor house. It was there that I came across all his freemason's documents and couldn't resist reading them.

A Nigerian Chieftain

One of the most memorable men I would meet in Swindon was an Igbo from Nigeria. His name was Leonard Ekechuwu and he was an ardent Catholic. He had trained as a caterer at Portsmouth Catering College, and they contacted us asking if we could give him work experience. He was an imposing figure, well over six feet tall, muscular and broad and extremely handsome. His English was impeccable. His apparent confidence took the customers in the Lounge Bar by surprise when we put him in there to gain bar experience. Many of the locals had never before met anyone with black skin and initially some behaved very badly towards him, but his charm and courtesy had them eating out of his hand before very long.

He was with us for a year and on returning to his homeland he kept in touch. He soon obtained a managerial post at Port Harcourt airport. However things were to change and not for the better. As was the case with so many other African nations, Nigeria was an artificial structure formed from former British colonies. No consideration was made for religious, linguistic and ethnic differences. The new country of sixty million people had almost three hundred differing ethnic and cultural groups – a recipe for disaster.

In July 1967 the Biafran war began when the south-eastern part of the country attempted secession as the Republic of Biafra. The Christian Igbo tribe was the most advanced and democratic of the groups and often resented by the other tribes. Unlike the other two main regions, decisions among the Igbo were made by a general assembly in which all men could participate. The causes of the Nigerian civil war were diverse, although some blamed the involvement of the British, Dutch, French and Italian oil companies whose battle for the rich Nigerian oilfields encouraged the civil war and kept it going until early 1970.

Initially the fight was between the two main tribes, the Hausas and the Igbos and by 1968 the Igbo area was surrounded. This lead to widespread starvation and many people died. In the spring of 1968 I received a letter from Leonard, smuggled out by a missionary, begging me to send parcels of food as his tribe were starving. I tried every means I could think of to do this. I contacted various church representatives but all replied that there was no chance of getting anything into the area. I sent off a reply but I realised there was little chance of it reaching him. I felt I had let him down.

Only in 1970 with the help of the British army, were the Igbo territories freed and the war ended. But although I tried to contact Leonard again then, there was no answer. I have never found out what happened to him.

Detective Superintendent George Gordon Smith

It was just after his retirement in 1962 that I first met Detective Superintendent George Gordon Smith. One autumn morning, two men entered the public bar of our hotel, The Duke, in the delightful Wiltshire village of Bratton. One of them was greeted by Harry Wheeler, a local farmer, with great gusto. Harry turned to me and said, 'Meet my friend, we grew up and went to school together, now he is famous. They call him Spycatcher!'

This was the man who had done more than anyone to ferret out spy rings, whether from Russia or Germany. He would become known as Britain's No.1 Spycatcher. His companion was a reporter from the *News Chronicle*, an old friend. George Smith frequently worked with the Press ensuring that reports gave away nothing which could damage police investigations and to make certain that everything appearing in the newspaper was correct.

These two men, together with Harry, joined us for lunch after the bar closed. 'Spycatcher' was careful not to reveal anything secret but I remember him saying, 'The middle classes of this country would be appalled if they knew what some members of Parliament and the peerage, as well as other well-known people have been doing.' He would not elaborate but added, 'Before long, you will know.' Three weeks later the whole scandal of the Profumo affair was revealed and the name Christine Keeler entered into the vocabulary as a scarlet woman. As well as spreading her sexual favours around the nobility she was also involved with a soon-to-be-discovered Russian spy.

George Smith, born in 1905, was the son of a farm labourer. When he was eight-years-old his father said to him, 'Boy, ya want to be a big strong man, don't ya? Well, 'ard work never 'urt no man and 'ee should start young.' Encouraged by his father, from the age of nine he was earning money on a milk round to augment his family's meagre income, receiving two shillings and sixpence a week for his efforts.

He worked hard and won a scholarship to Dauntsey's School, now a well-known public school. He became a boarder but it was hard for his family to provide any extras. His father would bake a large cake and cut it in slices and give it to George to sell to his companions and that would be his pocket money.

At fifteen, he passed the entrance examination for the RAF apprentices' training school but this sadly was discontinued after a few months. He decided to move to London, finding work as a pantry boy and later a footman. But thanks to a friendly police sergeant, at twenty-one, he was encouraged to join the police. That is when his unusual skills of detection emerged, and by thirty-seven he was a detective sergeant at Bow Street. He made his mark during the IRA terrorist attacks in 1929 and was seconded to Special Branch as a superintendent. During the war years, he unearthed many Nazi spy rings, working with MI5. One of his famous triumphs was his work with the Portland spy ring; the capture of Klaus Fuchs and the Krogers in Ruislip, earning the respect of President Hoover. Another success was unearthing the treachery of Burgess and Maclean in 1962; two of the Cambridge Four who spied for Russia. This was followed by his solving of the Vassall affair.

He would receive many further commendations. During his thirty-six years of service, he received twenty-two commendations from the Metropolitan Police Commissioners and he was awarded the Queen's Police Medal.

On retirement he went back to his roots and lived in our village until he died of a heart attack in 1970. He had kept accurate details of all his investigations and had planned to write his memoirs but died before the necessary time had passed before he could reveal them. He left them to his reporter friend, Norman Lucas, who published them in 1973.

Some Military Men and Dictators

We were offered the tenancy of a country inn in Bratton, Wiltshire. The Duke Hotel gave us the chance to run our own business and we were near enough to the Salisbury Plain to benefit from the activities of the School of Infantry nearby. This led to organising numerous dinners and cocktail parties for the officers. But the most interesting events occurred when Britain began training foreign armies in the 1960s. Groups of foreign officers would assemble on the Plain above our village and carry out manoeuvres. Many European armies would arrive – I remember the amazing uniforms of the Turkish in particular – but the majority would be from our one-time colonies. The personnel would range from subalterns to major generals. The Army Catering Corps would provide hay boxes filled with hot curries and rice and set them up in our forecourt. The participants then would sit in the bar to eat this delectable feast and hopefully order some beer to wash it down.

I could not understand why we would help foreign armies to train, teaching them modern methods of warfare. 'Quite simple,' said the Colonel when I confronted him. 'If we should ever have to fight them, we will know what they are going to do! We don't have to do the same.'

Clever, I thought.

He also told me that many of the African countries would send their best colonels and majors – and many of them subsequently would either take over the country as dictators or die in the attempt. So it was with great interest that I met the next regiment to arrive from Uganda. The major in charge walked into the lounge bar, nearly pushing me over in the process without a word of apology. He strode towards the counter and so doing, knocked his head on the low beams of the old inn. He swore, though not in English. It was, I learnt, Idi Amin.

He was an enormous man with broad shoulders and muscles like rugby balls and very hairy – not a pretty sight! He sat and had his meal brought to him by a British Private – and gave not a word of thanks – already he had the makings of a dictator. I watched his subsequent downfall with delight.

Captain Tom Clack RN and Commander Ken Frewer RN

During the 1960s whilst running the Duke at Bratton, many interesting and unusual people would come through the door. We never knew from one day to another who would be next. However, two of our regular customers who became our friends were also people who would leave a mark on all our lives. As they drank their glasses of beer, propped up at the counter, they would discuss the problems they were facing in an important project in which they were major players.

The project was the building and launch of the first of the Royal Navy's Resolution-class ballistic missile submarine. Captain Tom Clack, a long-serving submariner, was working for the Admiralty in a hotel in Bath which had been requisitioned for the Navy's use. He would spend his time commuting between there and Vickers shipbuilding site at the naval base at Faslane, overseeing its construction.

His colleague, another submariner and also a local resident, was appointed Port Captain of the first vessel. His fellow captain, titled Starboard, shared the command. There were two separate crews and each was destined to spend up to six months at a time submerged, while on patrol. When we worked in the bar, we could not fail to hear parts of their discussions. We lived through the problems encountered during the construction of the first ballistic weapon launcher. It was impossible not to recognise from their conversation and attitude, as they conversed, the good days and the bad days.

I had got to know the Maitre Chef at the Savoy Hotel, Silvino Trompetto. One day, Ken Frewer approached me asking for my help. He had been investigating the problems his crew might encounter while spending six months at sea and in cramped conditions. He realised one of the most important parts of the daily routine would be their mealtimes. He asked if I could arrange for him to meet Chef Trompetto to discuss the possibility of the senior chef on the vessel spending time in the Savoy kitchen, to learn how to improve the presentation of the meals, to make them more attractive and appetising for the crew.

'Tromps', as Silvino was affectionately nicknamed, was delighted to cooperate and the result was a great improvement in Navy 'grub'. An added bonus was that a spectacular cake was presented to the crew on its initial launch on 15th September 1967, in the presence of Queen Elizabeth, the Queen Mother.

My husband and I were later invited aboard to a party celebrating its commissioning in October of that year. Ken Frewer would remain in command for several years. The Resolution was finally decommissioned in October 1994 after sixty-nine patrols and remains laid up to this day in the Rosyth dockyard, with its reactor defuelled. Captain Clack moved on to subsequent construction and commissioning of succeeding submarines. Both of these officers had young families and I am sure their wives must have suffered much apprehension during those early days of nuclear warheads.

Lord Reith

It would not be long before another autocrat would step over the threshold – Lord Reith, once head of the British Broadcasting Corporation. He was using us as a staging post whilst visiting BBC Bristol. We were advised of his arrival and told he would require a private sitting room while he waited for transport to his next destination. He would need a pot of tea – Earl Grey, please – and smoked salmon sandwiches, with the crusts cut off. He was very tall, clean shaven and wearing a heavy black overcoat and Homburg hat. Looking over my head when he arrived, he said, 'You have your instructions?'

I took him to the residents' lounge – complete with its new notice 'PRIVATE' – and had Antonio, our Spanish waiter, take him his refreshment. He stayed with us for an hour, and left when the car arrived, leaving neither a tip for the waiter, nor a thank you.

More BBC Stars – Peter Cook and Dudley Moore

The next BBC arrivals were much more fun! We were asked to provide changing accommodation for the stars of a comedy programme called *Not Only... But Also*.

Although we had a television, the life of a hotelier gave little opportunity to watch it so I had no idea what to expect. When the film crew arrived on a busy morning in the bar, the customers were delighted to see Dudley Moore and Peter Cook emerging from the transport. I was surprised by how unkempt they both looked. Their hair was ruffled and straggly and they had obviously let their beards grow.

The producer asked if they could use one of our bedrooms for changing so of course I agreed. After about half an hour, the two comedians descended the stairs clad, to my great surprise, only in bearskins! This was to be their famous sketch on the Westbury White Horse during the Stone Age.

The sketch successfully filmed, they swiftly changed, complaining about feeling rather sore, having suffered a certain amount of discomfort climbing up and down the surface of the White Horse. Before long, they were relaxing with the customers in the lounge bar. Lovely people and not a drop of side with them, they gave me a kiss before leaving. Having shaved off the whiskers they wore as ancient Britons they looked quite different. I certainly made sure I saw that instalment on the television.

Feeding the Public – Louis Darsonval

Having worked as a hotelier for ten years, in 1957 I was interested to learn that the industry had decided to form a professional body, the Hotel and Catering Institute, now the Hotel and Industrial Management Association. We were notified that, for the first year only, direct entry would be granted to all hoteliers with at least eight years' experience. I applied but, to my disgust, was turned down because as a woman, the committee decided I took no active part in management but probably only did the flowers. They insisted I took the entrance examination, requiring four years at a catering college. This was a red rag to a bull. I informed them I would take the necessary examination in the six required subjects immediately. I did this and, to my delight, gained the highest marks in the country. Consequently I was admitted initially as an associate member. This led to my invitation to join the Cookery and Food Association and eventually to serve on the judging committee at Hotelympia for cookery competitions among the young students.

Among my fellow committee members were some of the greatest chefs and caterers of the era. Louis Darsonval was amongst them. Then maître chef at one of the most prestigious restaurants in London, he led the judging team. He would treat every dish with reverence, first looking at the presentation followed by tasting each ingredient on the plate. He wrote copious notes on each entry and after the winner was decided upon, he would give each competitor a short analysis of the pluses and minuses of his or her entry. He spurred them on with his enthusiasm.

Victor Ceserani

Victor Ceserani, another born teacher, was head of the catering section of Ealing Technical College. He said during an interview published in the *Caterer* that in 1934, aged fifteen, he told his parents he wanted to leave school and become a chef. His parents were supportive. His father, a wine waiter at the Ritz Hotel, spoke to the head chef Arséne Avignon who agreed to take him on as an apprentice. He earned seven shillings and sixpence (about thirty pence) a week supplying his own uniform and knives and working split duties from 9.30am to 2.30pm and 5pm to 9pm.

This tough life taught him the discipline of the kitchen. He recalls how a chef once asked him to make a hollandaise sauce, using twenty-four egg yolks. Not adroit at whisking eggs over the coal-fired stove, he ended up scrambling them. The chef de partie took the whole lot and threw it on the floor. He recalled, 'It made a lot of mess and I spent the rest of the day cleaning it up!'

He realised that a good apprenticeship in a busy kitchen cannot be replicated in a college. Three years later he moved to the Orleans Gentlemen's Club in St James as second chef. His initial training had paid off although he has since commented, 'There is no room in today's kitchens for the type of behaviour I experienced at the Ritz. M. Avignon imposed such rigorous standards of discipline that I thought he had missed his vocation and should have been a colonel in the French Foreign Legion!' However that was the way many top French kitchens were organised in those days.

He served with the Royal Fusiliers and the Army Catering Corps during the Second World War and on release took a course at a teacher training college. In 1951 he became a lecturer in professional cookery at Acton Technical College and was appointed Head of School for Hotel-keeping and Catering at Ealing College of Further Education in 1964. Meanwhile he wrote his manual, *Practical Cookery*, which is the bible for all young chefs even today, followed by his *Theory of Catering*. He received an MBE for his services to catering education in 1980. I will always regard it as a privilege to have met Vic. As a young hotelier with no formal training, he taught me so much.

Silvino Trompetto – Maître Chef at the Savoy

I met Silvino Trompetto when my son Clive began his five-year training in the kitchens at the Savoy Hotel. Although from an immigrant Italian family, Tromps, as he was known was the first British-born head chef at the Savoy.

Tromp took Clive under his wing during his training and although Clive would continue in management, cooking was always his favourite hobby. I met Tromps on many occasions, first when Clive started and then throughout the five-year scheme. Each year when I attended the Hotel and Catering Exhibition at Olympia, we would meet.

Trompetto told me about the terrible accident he'd had as a child. He was at the beach and he fell on a sand bucket. It must have been a heavy fall because the metal cut right through his nose and after surgery, it was completely removed and he had a false one built. This resulted in his voice having a strange nasal sound to it. He was brought up by an order of nuns, for whom he had the greatest respect.

I enjoyed his company and, even after he retired, we would keep in touch. Although a strict mentor, he was a master chef of the highest order and his teaching was the basis of many highly successful careers. I don't, however, think he had any inclination to train female chefs in his kitchen. Prue Leith reports that in 1975, she approached him asking for a two week trial for a female graduate of her newly opened School of Food and Wine. She fully expected to be told the 'usual nonsense' about girls taking men's mind off the job. But his excuse for not allowing a female in his kitchen left her speechless: 'Because, dear lady, at a certain time of the month, women cause the mayonnaise to curdle.' My personal impression on meeting him was that he had other ideas on the uses of women.

Christopher Pollard – Teacher, Caterer, Hotelier, entrepreneur par excellence

Invited to act as a judge at Hotelympia in 1960 for the Junior Salon

Culinaire, I met someone who became important in my life. The competition was for the best international buffet presentation and the winners were a team of six students from Ealing Technical College. These six students were paraded before us and congratulated on the high standard of their entry. Among them was one young man, confident and well turned out, who on being introduced to 'Mrs Eileen Younghusband', was clearly heard to say, 'Not that ***** woman!' It seemed that after I was awarded the Sir Francis Towle Gold Medal the previous year, for gaining the highest marks in the Hotel and Catering Institute's entry examination, my name had been bandied about by the lecturers as someone who had succeeded without going to college. Consequently, with my unusual surname, I was easily recognised.

Christopher Pollard is the epitome of a perfect entrepreneur. He had vision, was a perfectionist and a great networker but, above all, had the wisdom to marry a delightful fellow student, Vivien. Chris is always impeccably dressed and charming and the most gracious host it has been my luck to encounter. Vivien is the perfect foil for him. Her artistic flair in presentation and her shrewd mind together with her ability to act as the 'checks and balances' in the partnership helped make their career path a fantastic success. After a short time teaching in a Cardiff college, they were offered the chance to buy a hotel in Barry. Within a short time the Mount Sorrel Hotel was the leading hotel in the area, hosting the most important functions. This success led them to look farther afield. Chris explored the possibility of providing catering services in the Middle East and successfully negotiated a contract to provide school meals (only for boys of course) in Saudi Arabia. It is there he made his name which led to further contracts in the area.

In the meantime, his company Hamard Catering was providing services for all the major events in Cardiff and elsewhere in Wales, including for visiting royalty. Moving into industrial catering, he became a major influence in the country until bought out by Grand Metropolitan industrial division, the Compass Group.

In recognition of the increased employment he had brought to Wales and his charity works, he was awarded the OBE. Despite not being Welsh, he had the honour of serving as High Sheriff for South Glamorgan in between 1988 and 1989.

In future years, when Peter and I retired as hoteliers, we acted as catering consultants for many different companies. On several occasions, we would work with Chris's company when they undertook the catering for the Welsh Eisteddfods and the Farnborough Air Show.

Fred Parker

In the late 1950s I stood for election as an Urban District Councillor under the banner 'Vote Younghusband for a Progressive Ventnor.' I was elected, to find myself the only woman amongst nine men on the Council. Once more I had to assert myself since they would have already made their decisions at Rotary or Masonic meetings! Women were still fighting to be listened to in the 1950s. This was my first introduction to local and national politics.

Fred Parker was a long-time member of Bratton's Parish Council. Fred was born in Tonypandy and was Welsh to the core. He bore many similarities to another resident, George Thomas; including a strong facial resemblance. One would be certain he was Labour. He had started life working in the coal mines of South Wales, later transferring to the local Parks Department. He worked hard and became a specialist in horticulture. A Bratton landowner managed to prevail upon him to leave Wales and come and look after her large estate and gardens. After working and getting to know Fred, she became an ardent Labour supporter and Fred became a Wiltshire fixture. As a local councillor, he did a lot for the village and although always pro-Labour, he never let that influence his efforts to support what was best for Bratton residents. He never lost his Welsh accent and would always lead the singing with his rich alto voice in convivial evenings in the public bar. Mattie his wife, our barmaid, was the rich source of delicious Welsh cakes! Together the Parker family contributed a lot to village life.

Monks and Rotarians

Amongst our regular guests in Wiltshire were two monks from Downside Abbey who found us in the *Good Food Guide*. I have usually found Catholic clerics to be both ardent gastronomes and expert wine-bibbers! Father Theodore and Father Benet were no exception. Having found us, they became regular customers, especially when they discovered a collection of fine 'bin ends' of wine, kept for special customers in my office. They were in there like a shot making their selection.

Both very good conversationalists, they became great friends of ours. My husband Peter had been brought up in a Catholic family and attended one of their famous boarding schools. So they were amused to find he had married someone with Huguenot ancestry and immediately christened me as 'the heretic friend'. I enjoyed their company immensely.

Both had been teachers at Downside College but were now retired from academic life and occupied in pastoral care. They were two quite different characters. Father Benet, tall and lean, taught Biology and Zoology and had spent some time at a monastery in San Diego County, U.S.A., while recovering from tuberculosis. There he had spent his time converting the native Indians, travelling on a donkey to their settlements out in the desert. Father Theodore, a rather tubby figure, was an Oxford scholar and a classicist, teaching Greek and Latin. He was horrified to learn I only spoke French and German and had no knowledge of Latin.

On one occasion they invited us to a special Rotary dinner held at Wells Cathedral. They had been put in charge of doling out the wine to the guests from the cache provided from the members' cellars. Father Benet stood at one of the desks and underneath were hidden the vintage bottles he had kept back for his special friends. Needless to say, we got first choice.

During another occasion, when we joined them for lunch, they caused consternation when they brought up the subject of birth control during the meal. They both had voices that carried to the farthest corners of the room and to the amazement, and perhaps amusement, of the nearby guests they put forward their views on the alternative methods of contraception.

I kept in touch with them after we gave up the Duke in 1970 and moved to the Court Farmhouse. Whenever they came to dinner, they expected the same standard as the *Good Food Guide* dictated. However, the elder one, Theodore, died very soon afterwards. But Father Benet was constantly in touch.

Spanish Connections

From 1960, when we took over the Duke at Bratton, we had always employed Spanish waiters from Las Mercedes Hotel in the then newly popular Andalusian village of Torremolinos. Aged between eighteen and thirty-five, they came for six months to learn or improve their English. We went through a couple of Manolos, a Diego, Leonardo and two Pepés. They were charming, hardworking and delightful – mostly from very humble backgrounds but taking advantage of the boom in the growth of tourism in their homeland to improve their lot.

The very first one to arrive, Antonio Barranco was the oldest and nearest my age. He was also the most accomplished, not only an excellent waiter but also a great cook. He taught me how to make authentic paella, just as his mother had made. His English was comprehensible and not only was he a comic – almost a spitting image of Norman Wisdom – but he excelled in the art of origami. He created the most incredible Christmas decorations from brown paper and paper napkins which we used to decorate the bars through the festive season.

He was the customers' favourite and mine too. All too soon his six months was up and we had to say goodbye. He had originally arrived by train from Spain but I insisted he returned by air. He was terrified so I decided to take a well-earned break and booked to return with him. To make matters worse for him, we were travelling on the 13th of the month, which fell on a Tuesday and, as we left the inn, a black cat walked across his path – all signs of impending bad luck in Spain. I tried to pacify him by telling him that for us it had to be a Friday for bad luck on the 13th, that black cats were lucky in England and that since we were flying to British Gibraltar that luck should still apply. It worked – he relaxed and enjoyed the trip. I kept in touch with him throughout the years, either visiting Torremolinos or writing to him until our friendship came to a sudden end. His wife found my letters, written in English which she could not understand and immediately accused him of philandering, banning any further contact. What a shame!

Señor Orbegozo – A Basque Steel Manufacturer

In order to understand my Spanish staff, I took a concentrated course of private lessons in their language. My teacher, Brian Steel, was the Spanish master at a nearby boys' public school. In around twenty lessons, I learnt the basics and continued to improve over the years, practicing with the boys. This would lead to a strange confrontation.

I usually tried to give each Spanish waiter experience of larger hotels and would take them on a day off to visit the Goddard Arms, where some of my old staff still remembered me. I was having lunch there with Pepé Cubero, when the waitress came to me and said, 'I could hear you talking Spanish. There are two guests here who do not speak a word of English and they are looking for help. Could you assist them? I think they are having coffee in the lounge.' Of course I agreed and we went in search of them, eventually tracking them down to their bedroom.

Completely forgetting the magic siesta time, I knocked on the door. '*Quien está?*' came the voice, 'Who is it?' I replied in my best Spanish: 'A friend of Spain'. I was told to come in and there, in bed, were the Spanish couple. They appeared to be in their sixties and both were wearing woollen caps on their head; I guess they were feeling the winter chill.

Rather nonplussed, I apologised and introduced myself and the young man by my side, who was looking extremely embarrassed. I said I had been told that they were asking for some help. The man introduced himself as Señor Orbegozo and told me that he owned a large steel manufacturing factory in Hernani in the Basque area. He had been buying scrap metal from a dealer in Swindon who, after the first delivery, had begun inserting lumps of concrete in the bales of scrap steel, increasing the weight and defrauding the buyer. Naturally, when this was discovered, action had to be taken. So this Spanish gentleman had come over to Britain to find a lawyer to take the dealer to court. But since few people those days spoke Spanish, he needed an interpreter to help. He asked me to act in this capacity but I did not think my Spanish sufficiently good for the task so I arranged for my teacher, Brian Steel, to take over. There was a satisfactory outcome and Señor Orbegozo was eventually compensated.

Thinking that was the end of the affair, I dismissed it from my mind. You can imagine my surprise when coming down the stairs one morning into the lounge bar of our hotel, I found the Spanish couple talking to Pepé. I asked whether all was well. 'Oh yes,' was the reply, 'I am so grateful to you for your help. But I have come to talk to you about something else!' He went on to say he thought I was a good businesswoman and asked if I would become his purchasing agent for scrap metal in Britain. Taken aback at first, I recovered and asked for more details. He told me he would pay my airfare to come to San Sebastian to sign a contract witnessed by the British Consul there. I pulled my thoughts together and asked how many tons he wanted to purchase. The reply staggered me. He wanted 4,000 tons each month, with commission of fourteen shillings for every ton. That would convert to £2,800 a month, in today's money, a considerable sum in 1967. Always willing to have a go, I agreed.

The following day I wondered what I had let myself in for. But within a week, my bank manager rang and told me a letter of credit had been deposited in my bank for £120,000! My credit rating shot up! Back to reality, I started exploring how I could find this amount of scrap steel.

I remembered that in Swindon, I had done a special favour for the managing director of Pressed Steel. Ringing him, I reminded him that I had helped him arrange a secret meeting with Communist trade union leaders without the Press knowing and asked if he could help me. To my surprise he offered me a thousand tons a month of Number 4 bales of clean off-cuts. After investigating possible means to transport vast amounts of steel scrap, I prepared for my trip to Spain. In a beautiful hotel in the attractive town of San Sebastian the deal was signed. I reported my initial results and returned home ready for the fray.

John Lowenstein and Jean Braconnier

Recalling that the son of a close friend of the family was currently the chairman of the Chamber of Shipping, I enrolled his help. He put me in touch with John Lowenstein, the owner of a scrap steel exporting company, based in Dagenham. When I rang his number, he sounded more than surprised to hear some woman from the heart of Wiltshire asking if he would be interested in joining her in exporting scrap steel to a factory in Spain. I had no idea of his age or background but he sounded young and very sure of himself.

He suggested I travel to London and meet him at a well-known restaurant to discuss the matter, stipulating that I carry a copy of *The Times* under my arm – just like you read about in spy novels. I encountered a dapper young man, obviously Jewish, elegantly dressed. He took charge and ushered me into the building, pointing out that he was very well-known at this establishment and we would be extremely well looked after. We descended the long wide staircase and there at the bottom was the restaurant manager, very smart in his morning suit, beaming with a smile from ear to ear.

John Lowenstein turned to me, 'You see what a good customer I am here.' At that moment, the young manager threw his arms around my neck and said with a strong French accent, 'Allo, Madame Young'usban, how wonderful to see you.' It was Jean Braconnier, who had been sent to us at the Goddard Arms in Swindon some years earlier for training. Needless to say, we *were* very well looked after. My stock went up considerably with my new scrap metal partner. He agreed to work with me and did well out of it, getting a large portion of the commission. We successfully carried on trading with Spain for a further three years until General Franco changed the rules. The Basque region and especially Hernani, where the steel factory was located, had a strong Separatist following and was a constant thorn in Franco's flesh. Export of scrap metal had been restricted to permit holders of export licences, issued by Margaret Thatcher's government. Franco decreed all importers must also obtain an import licence from the Spanish authorities and none were ever issued to businesses located in Basque territory. That was the death knell to our enterprise.

Major General Christopher Man and the Break-In

In 1968 after a particularly busy and stressful time at the inn, Peter had a nervous breakdown. It was not surprising. We had taken no holiday nor a single day off for over two years. The inn was always busy and the clientele demanding. His doctor advised him to take a break away from the business. Reluctantly he agreed and went to Bude to stay with old friends from our West Country days.

By then I had a young assistant chef and a very competent Spanish waiter so I thought I could cope. It was August and the weekend when the village held their renowned pram race. This year, as usual, entries came from villages all around. The race started in front of the *Duke*. It was expected to be our busiest day of the year and we had ordered in extra stock in preparation.

The morning dawned and I got up early to prepare the trays of tea to be delivered to the residents. The house was full. I entered the kitchen and went through to the room where we kept the stores, but the door wouldn't budge. Something was wedged behind it. It felt soft – almost like a body. I pushed harder and eventually it yielded.

The door had been wedged shut by a large sack of detergent. I knew something was seriously wrong. All dry supplies were usually kept in an outer laundry room. Then I saw the back window was smashed. The wine cellar door had been forced open and the entire stock of spirits and cigarettes was gone, plus several of the small metal barrels of beer; the extra stock for the busiest day of the year had been stolen.

I would have expected our black Labrador to have given a warning of a break-in, but the thieves were well-prepared. I saw through the window the dog lying on the floor in his run. I thought he was dead but fortunately he moved his head. They had thrown him some doped food and he was lying comatose just outside his kennel.

By now the guests were in the dining room waiting to order breakfast. I asked Manolo to take over, explaining to them what had happened, I asked if they would mind making do with cereal and fruit on this occasion. Thank goodness they agreed. I rang the police and then the emergency number for the brewery. I ordered what replacement stock I imagined we would need and then went to meet the staff. The three barmaids were looking to restock their shelves – I told them to be patient.

Fortunately the brewery came up trumps and a delivery arrived in under an hour. Order was restored. The staff worked like mad to get everything ready for service.

The customers, all keen to see the start of the race, were pouring into the bars. I greeted them and then we went outside and watched as the chairman of the village council fired the starting pistol to begin the race. The participants, all in fancy dress and comic gear, set off up the hill to the Westbury White Horse. I had a breathing space to gather my wits. But it did not last long; the police arrived and they wanted all the details and a list of the losses. I did my best.

And then the prams returned helter skelter! I presented the winner with his prize. The bar filled up and it was all hands to the pump! Finally things quietened down. I leaned over the bar exhausted. It was then Major General Man entered and came over to me. He had taken over about a month before as the Officer-in-Charge of the Army Commissions Board in Westbury, where potential officers were put through their paces. He lived in the village with his wife and had come in on a few occasions for a quiet beer. I barely knew him. He put his arm around my shoulder and said, 'And what about you, how are you feeling?' He had sized up the situation seeing the police there and he was the only person who had thought to check on how I was coping.

I don't cry – not even when my husband died beside me a few years later, or when I heard the news from my brother at 3 o'clock in the morning that my beloved Clive, my only child, had suddenly died in Texas. But I did then. I wept and wept with tiredness, frustration and with anger that I had to cope alone. That is how Christopher Man became a special person in my life. When Peter returned in improved health, he too became a friend of his, but mine was a very special friendship.

Chris Man's life since the outbreak of war had been far from wonderful. He was a full-time soldier, serving as a Major in the Middlesex Regiment. Sent out to Hong Kong, he was captured by the Japanese and put in a prison camp and like so many others sent to build the Burma railway. He had married Topsy as she was nicknamed, who had also been in Hong Kong working as a nurse. When the Japanese took over, she had also been imprisoned in a harsh women's prison like that so movingly portrayed in the BBC programme, *Tenko*. They had no communication with each other during their whole period of incarceration and no idea whether either had survived. Finally released in the August of 1945, Chris was put on a sailing ship on a long and slow journey home. Walking round the many decks after about ten days at sea, he came across a group of released female prisoners. To his utter amazement, Topsy was amongst them.

Home and still in the Army, he volunteered for training as a paratrooper at thirty-six years of age. He was the only ex-prisoner of war to become a member of the Parachute Regiment but that was his character – brave and willing to tackle anything. His abilities earned him rapid promotion and now here he was for his final role, overseeing the Army Commissions Board at Westbury.

Sadly the years of imprisonment had had a terrible effect on his wife. She suffered brain damage and underwent considerable surgery which left her in a poor state. She needed constant care and was unable to fulfil the social duties of a senior army officers' wife. This made it hard for General Man.

Peter, too, was never the same man after his illness and would suffer his first heart attack very soon after we had retired from being full-time hoteliers. Chris and I would often meet and talk about our losses. He led a lonely life. As the most senior officer at the Commissions Board and dealing mostly with young potential officers, he had to keep apart from them in order to give an unbiased and true assessment of their worth and not be swayed by personal relationships.

There were few permanent officers on the base and he lived away from the Officers' Mess in a house in our village. Peter and I could rarely both leave the hotel together – our life was long hours and hard work – so if there was ever a free moment, I would drive up to the Salisbury Plain, only a short distance from the village. Often Chris and I would meet and walk together through the quiet fields and share our problems. He was the kindest of men, tall and fit and with a great sense of humour.

Those afternoon meetings would help me get through the unending days of dealing with difficult customers or staff shortages. I think I helped him too in coping with an increasingly sick wife, who was unable to support him in the many activities he had to attend. When we sold the hotel and retired to a lovely old house in the village, he was constantly at hand to help. Sadly when he retired from the army, his wife wanted to return to her birthplace in Scotland. We made one visit up there to see him before he died. It was a great loss to me. I often see him in my mind's eye on his bicycle, that bore the single star of a Major General, as he came for his daily glass of beer with his lovely black Labrador, Butch – this tall, extremely good-looking military man, with an unforgettable twinkle in his eye.

Mickey Martin and the Dambusters

From the first days of taking over our own hotel in Wiltshire, members of the Royal Air Force would once more enter our lives. One evening a group of men in their forties arrived in the bar. They were already in a happy mood. Before long they learned that Peter and I were both ex-RAF and of course a party began. They decided to stay the night. I found to my astonishment, that it was a reunion group of the remnants of the crews of the Dambusters, led by Micky Martin.

He was one of several Anzac pilots in the raid and together with Shannon, a fellow Aussie, they were two of the most colourful personalities of the Dambusters squadron. Martin, who flew a Lancaster famously known as P for Popsy – the wartime slang for a good sort (female!) – was a highly respected bomber pilot before he was seconded to 617 Squadron for the special mission. A laconic character, he had a reputation for flying the bombers at dangerously low levels. To avoid flak – anti-aircraft gunfire – he would fling his Lancaster around like a Spitfire. He was eventually recognised as one of the best RAF bomber pilots of the Second World War.

To meet him in these happy surroundings was a joy and before long, once the bar closed, we were all engaged in some of the games we used to play in the Mess to relieve tension. On this occasion, we armed ourselves with folded newspapers and, whilst blindfolded, crawled around the floor scoring hits on each other, the loser buying the next round. We were all back in wartime for a short while.

Family Connections

My Brother Dennis, Space Scientist and Engineer at NASA's Jet Propulsion's Laboratory

Dennis was four years younger than I was and my total opposite in many ways. He was destined to be a scientist and engineer. Whereas I would always act on impulse, he would give a much more considered judgement. I loved sport; for him it was boring. I was intensely patriotic; whereas Dennis was more a world citizen. Since I went abroad to work in France when I was barely seventeen, and then was evacuated with the company I worked for before joining the WAAF, I missed a lot of his maturing years. I do know however how proud the whole family has been of him and his contribution to science.

Dennis always had the ability to command respect. The friendships he made at school continued throughout his life, despite the miles between so many of his pals. He was organised, neat and always in control of his emotions. As a child he had wavy hair (to my envy as mine was dead straight). He must have been attractive as he had several girlfriends in his youth, some of whom would keep in contact with him over the years. I never heard of anyone who disliked him. He loved travelling to foreign countries and I have enjoyed many trips with him throughout Europe.

Like me, he left school at sixteen. He had taken several evening courses pursuing his interest in radio and physics, while being employed at Cosmos Manufacturing Company where they specialised in radio valves. He had hoped these courses could be used towards a degree. He was then called up in 1945 to do his two years of National Service, in

87

the RAF, training as an electrician. During those two years, he studied for an external degree with Imperial College. Despite the difficulties of fitting in his studies, he was successful and gained his B.Sc.

He went on to lecture at Southampton University while working on his Ph.D and researching Geiger counters. In the 1950s he moved to the USA to a lecturing post at Kansas University. After several university positions, both lecturing and conducting research, he moved to California to work on the unmanned space programme. He was responsible for the development of the instruments on the Surveyor probes, designed to evaluate lunar conditions prior to the manned Apollo landings. After one successful Apollo landing, the astronauts walked over to the Surveyor, disconnected the television camera and Dennis received it back for testing!

He would be involved in the design of several further unmanned spacecraft instruments. Seven Mariner missions were sent successfully to Mars. Voyagers 1 and 2 were launched in 1977 to take advantage of a favourable planetary alignment. Designated to study just Jupiter and Saturn, unexpectedly the probes were able to continue their mission into the outer solar system. Voyager 1 is now the farthest human-made object from Earth, and is still travelling. It has recently been reported as having left the solar system. Two of the instruments on this probe Dennis designed.

When the unmanned space programme was terminated and a space station was set up, Dennis contributed to the planning of which instruments would be onboard. Later his duties changed and reverted to his earlier experience with bio-medical engineering. Together with Dick Heyser, a specialist in loud-speaker technology, he researched ultrasound diagnostics with its many uses in medicine. His final post was as head of the Department for the Search for Extraterrestrial Life, sending out mathematical signals into space, hoping one day for a response. He told me it could not be expected before the arrival of my grandchild's great-great-grandchildren – if then.

Of all the duties he undertook, he was probably proudest of his ultrasound work, notably on the Cardiology Advisory Committee of NHLBI Institute of the National Institute of Health, and his work in Egypt as US project director working for the National Science Foundation at Cairo University, the first use of medical ultrasonic imaging in an Arab country.

It was shortly after that he suggested Peter and I might like to join him in the States after we had retired from hotel keeping. As Dennis was an American citizen, my husband and I would be allowed in under the Fifth Preference and issued with the much-valued Green Cards, allowing us to work there. We decided to try this but I know he was very disappointed when after a couple of years, we decided that American life was not for us and we returned to Britain.

On retirement, my brother moved to his favourite part of California – Carlsbad, near San Diego. He had always enjoyed writing but the last few years of his working life were spent writing formal proposals for research funds into health diagnostic equipment. Now he could indulge his desire to write about less esoteric subjects. He had many articles published in magazines covering computers, local affairs etc. Many of them were humorous; Dennis had a delicious off-beat sense of humour, but he really wanted to write fiction. Finally he wrote his first mystery novel and had found a publisher. The sad thing was he never saw it published. He died of lung cancer after only a short illness in 2003. For someone who had never smoked, it was a cruel end to a life which had contributed so much to the common good.

Dennis always underplayed his part in the Space Race. As Jill, his wife says, 'Dennis was never one of the world's politicians and did not brag about his activities.' Consequently he was never sufficiently recognised for his solid work as a scientist or his teaching ability. However those who worked with him knew and appreciated him for his insight and ability to get to the heart of problems. He contributed so much to medical research and left the world a better place.

Ed Chandler and Other Space Boffins

During my stay in California, I would meet several of my brother's colleagues at the Jet Propulsion Laboratory. Ed Chandler was especially close to my brother. He had a strong East coast accent and a beautiful singing voice. He had started life as a radio announcer in his home town.

He was Dennis's leading engineer and he later left the space programme to become manager of the local branch of Radio Shack – retailers of all things electronic made by the Tandy Company of Texas. It was through him that, during my stay in the United States, I went to work in that store with him at La Crescenta.

He assured me that my knowledge of Radar would be an asset. To work in a shop specialising in electronics and high-tech articles, and patronised by space scientists, was a little overwhelming since I knew little about the technical side. I wondered if I would justify his faith in me. However, it transpired that common sense was more important. Since we were so near the JPL, many of our customers would come from this highly specialised community; they would arrive clutching some device or other that was not working and ask me to look at it. I would always start at the beginning and say, 'Let's check the contacts,' and sure enough, most times it was as simple as that. Either the plug was not connected correctly or the wiring was loose. They went away satisfied.

Among other boffins I met at my brother's get-togethers was a German who had come over after the war, at the same time as Werner von Braun. He was working on the mass spectrometer. His name was Hans Böttger, a very formal man – I expected him to click his heels when we were introduced. I had not realised his wartime background, but during a conversation he casually mentioned he was a submariner during the war and commander of a U-boat. He went on to say how once he found himself in the English Channel in a fog and was going up the Thames. He admitted he had quickly skedaddled! He also told me how many of our merchant vessels he had destroyed. I had only one response – that I had served with the RAF and Fighter Command, but I never mentioned how many bombers we had shot down.

Don Schroeder, another Jet Propulsion colleague of my brother, a slight, dapper man, was brought up in Arkansas, a state of treeless plains where many German immigrants originally settled, many moving at the time of the Gold Rush to the West. Don acted as negotiator for the purchase and manufacture of the instruments. He helped to keep all the projects on time and on budget, including the great telescope in Hawaii. He was renowned as a nit-picker *par excellence*. It was said if Schroeder approved something, you knew it was the best money could buy. Since his retirement, I have met him many times and he is still searching for the best buy, whether it is his latest car – he owns several – his TV or his clothes, the Schroeder beady eye always gets a good deal. He has never married and lives a solitary life reading his *Wall Street Journal* and checking his investments.

Mel Smoekler was another close colleague of my brother. Married to a first generation Italian lady, he spoke her language perfectly and was a great host and of course his wife produced fantastic Italian dishes. I always loved my visits to his house.

Most of these brilliant men were, at first appearance, fairly unremarkable and often quiet and withdrawn. As I got to know them better, they would open up, and represented an amazing cross-section of American life, with family connections from so many countries.

Clive – My Only Son and a Very Special Person

My son Clive was born on the day my husband was demobbed from the RAF on 27 March 1946. He seemed to have a smile on his face from the moment of his birth. His sunny disposition stayed with him until he died a few days after his fiftieth birthday, when part of my heart died with him too.

His life was never a normal one. He moved schools five times before he was seven years old due to our constant transfer from management of one hotel to another. It was then we decided that if our home was not to be static, his school should be and he was sent to a preparatory school in Reading run by the Presentation Brothers. Being a Catholic establishment, it was only for boys. Like his father, he never was good at mathematics but this disadvantage was overcome as soon as he mastered computer skills. Years later, he asked why we moved so often. I explained that after the war, life was changing constantly and coming back to civilian life after years in the services was difficult; you had to take whatever opportunities presented themselves. I hope he understood.

Despite not being a keen scholar, he excelled in other ways. He was always the leader and despite only getting one General School Certificate, he won the leadership cup on the Isle of Wight for a strenuous endurance record over a long weekend organised by the Boy Scouts' Association. He always had many friends and kept them. He decided he wanted to leave school at sixteen and train to be a hotelier like us.

One of our previous staff was now the banqueting manager at the renowned Savoy Hotel so I asked whether he could arrange for Clive to join their prestigious management training scheme. He was accepted on the condition he gained a year's experience elsewhere until he was eighteen. Since we were employing and training waiters from the Spanish hotel Las Mercedes in Torremolinos, the manager there was happy to take him on. So, at almost seventeen, he travelled alone to southern Spain. He did not speak a word of the language but although his previous teachers had made him drop French, saying he would never become a linguist, within three months he was speaking fluent Spanish, coloured no doubt by the local dialect. He soon learned to cook, wait and work in reception and returned a year later, confident and capable.

Five years training at the Savoy was far more difficult than studying a university course. He worked for two years in the kitchens, doing split shifts over ten hours a day, for six days a week. He then spent a year as a commis waiter, carrying all the dishes from the kitchen to the tables and often returning home with his feet bleeding. After six months spent learning bar work and six months in the banqueting suite, he finally spent the final year in reception learning the art of dealing with the public and coping with every query and problem imaginable. He came out of this comprehensive training with an excellent reference and a great deal of knowledge. He had met people from every walk of life, from immigrants working in the kitchens to film stars such as Bing Crosby who would practice his golfing shots along the hotel corridors, and Elizabeth Taylor who was regularly wined and dined by her many admirers.

He told me the most memorable day was the funeral of Sir Winston Churchill, a regular client of the Savoy. He saw the coffin being carried down the river in the Royal Barge. That day the waiters who always served him reserved his usual table in his memory and together paid for his favourite dish to be served – pâté de foie gras.

After five years he was ready for his first management post. This was at the North British Hotel in Edinburgh. A year later, he joined our friend Chris Pollard as general manager for his outside catering firm, Hamard Catering. He gained experience in mass event catering at the Welsh Eisteddfod, agricultural shows and royal events; by now he had a very rounded experience. He worked hard and he played hard; he was a keen water-skier and had his first serious girlfriend. Even now, I meet people who remember his days spent in South Wales.

Everything changed when my brother suggested Clive spend a year in the USA. Clive, always ready for a new experience, was off like a shot. He had a year's permit to stay. Not legally permitted to work there, he still managed to get a hotel management position at the Indian Wells Hotel in Palm Desert, where the Bob Hope Golf Tournament took place annually. After this year's experience he returned home and was quickly offered a management post in Johannesburg. It may seem he moved about a lot but it is quite normal in the hotel industry, to get as much experience as possible in the early years. However, the situation in South Africa became more and more difficult as the apartheid regime was coming under fire. We visited him in the winter of 1975 and I hated every moment over there.

It was the following year when Peter and I decided to take up my brother's offer and try life in the USA. We were given residency status, and within a year we managed to secure this for Clive also. He was appointed reservations manager for the newly opened New Otani hotel in Los Angeles, owned by a Japanese company, where he met up with John Layzell, who would become his closest friend and later his best man. Two years later Clive was appointed as the general manager of a new hotel in East Hollywood where he would meet his future wife, Liz, a Canadian nurse. His success there would lead to him being headhunted to run a famous establishment in Chicago.

The century-old Chicago Athletics Association and Gentlemen's Club was sited on the banks of Lake Michigan in the heart of this great city. This would be Clive's greatest challenge and his greatest achievement. There were only eleven such highly rated clubs in the USA and among the members were top academics, medical specialists, businessmen, actors and politicians. It was where the President might stay when visiting the city. We visited him frequently and loved the city with its vibrant waterfront and amazing skyscrapers.

The Chicago club needed a new look and this was his task. Before long, his Savoy expertise managed to raise the standard. There was a new French chef, improved accommodation and altogether a more successful business. His daughter was born in 1980 and spent her early childhood there. He stayed there for eleven years and organised the celebrations for the centenary of the club. By then everything was running smoothly and he was looking for a new challenge.

It was then he was approached by the Fort Worth Club in Texas. They offered him a three-year contract and an increased salary. After visiting, he could see a lot needed improving but he felt ready for a change so agreed to go. In retrospect, this was a wrong decision since he did not then understand the Texan mentality. However the family moved there in 1991. They found a lovely house and all seemed well. Before long Clive had found an excellent chef and improved the menu choices; the membership increased considerably, winning back many old members who had become disillusioned under the previous management. He inaugurated a sporting club, extending activities to cover game shooting and fishing, both of which were favourite hobbies of his.

Fort Worth had started life as a frontier town and was fortified against the threats of Native Americans from the border with Mexico. The club was sited in the centre of this old town, whose fortune had been made on cattle breeding and, later, silver mining. It was named in honour of General William Jenkins Worth who built ten forts to mark the west Texan frontier.

The club owned a seven-storey building and part of its activities consisted of letting business premises. This was undertaken by a business manager who became a friend of Clive's, or so he thought. At the end of three years, Clive's contract was due to be renewed. In Chicago, this would have been discussed and renewed some time before the contract expired, but things were different in Texas. He heard nothing from the Board. He was to learn that Texans prefer to have their fellow Texans running things. They called Clive in and thanked him for all his efforts and told him that as it was running so successfully, they would now put in the Texan Building Manager to run the whole operation at a lower salary. Clive was offered three months' salary in lieu of notice and that was that. When I learned of this, I was anxious – he was fifty and I knew that it was always harder at that age to find new positions of equal seniority.

He had to sell his house and start looking for another job. Few posts of similar stature were advertised so eventually he decided to join an English friend from his youth who was living in Washington State and set up a business organising gastronomic tours to Britain. By then Peter, his father, had died and he had received a small inheritance. He invested this in the business and he started making plans. But once again fate stepped in and Clive's partner's wife left him. The divorce settlement took all the money Clive had invested in the business. His friend initially started to repay him but then disappeared owing a large sum.

The strain on Clive was enormous. He finally managed to get another management job, this time running a golf resort and hotel. The salary was smaller but it was in Florida and housing prices were lower. I felt relieved. The family moved to Sarasota, initially renting a house. Clive took up his post on the Monday. I decided to wait until the Sunday before I phoned him, to see how things had gone. On the Saturday he was due to sign the papers for the purchase of his new home. At about three o'clock on the Sunday morning, which was 10 o'clock the previous evening in Florida, my telephone rang, waking me up. It was my brother – his words to me I will never forget: 'Eileen I have some very bad news for you. Clive has died.'

It took me a few seconds to take it in. I went cold. Clive had been under considerable strain, brought on by the events which had occurred, and had bottled it up. Never one for going to the doctor, he had ignored some warning signs. The worry, then the relief at finding a job after some months, had been too much for his body to take. He had suffered a brain haemorrhage. Taken to hospital, they had worked on him for an hour but it was hopeless. I had lost my only child.

Freddie Laker

My journey to Clive's funeral in Florida passed in a trance but I will never forget the kindness and consideration of Freddie Laker. I was flying on his airline and it coincided with a day when he was taking the same flight. My cousin Beau pointed him out to me as we arrived at Gatwick. As I took my seat, he was helping people put their luggage on the rack. As mine was a late booking for seats reserved for bereavement flights, he came over immediately to help me. After take-off, he joined me and spent two hours comforting me and producing a bottle of wine and pouring me a glass. He then helped me alight at Miami and saw me through the protocol there until I met my brother. I will always remember his consideration which helped alleviate the pain of such a journey. On my return home, he phoned me from his base in the UK to see how I was – he was a man who cared.

'Van' Cliburn – Pianist Extraordinaire

Amongst the bad memories of Fort Worth and Texas, there remains one good one. It was meeting with the world-famous pianist Harvey Lavan Cliburn Junior, known to all as 'Van'. Born in 1934 in Louisiana, this American pianist showed an amazing musical talent from an early age. Originally he was taught by his mother, Rildia Bee O'Bryan, herself a great pianist, who had been taught by Arthur Friedheim, a pupil of Franz Liszt. By the age of twelve he had won a state-wide piano competition leading to a debut performance with the Houston Symphony Orchestra.

After training at the Juilliard School of Music, he entered the first International Tchaikovsky Competition in 1958. This event had been designed to display Soviet cultural superiority after their technological success with the Sputnik launch the previous year. His performance of Tchaikovsky's Piano Concerto No. 1 and Rachmaninoff's Piano Concerto No. 3 was outstanding, earning him a standing ovation from the audience lasting eight minutes. When it was time to announce the winner, the judges, nonplussed, decided to ask permission of the Soviet leader to award it to a non-Russian. Khrushchev asked, 'Is he the best?' Returning home victorious, Van Cliburn was given the first-ever ticker-tape parade in New York accorded to a classical musician. His success led him to international fame. This led to the inauguration of a quadrennial piano competition which now equals in repute the Tchaikovsky Piano Competition in Russia.

How did I meet this genius? He was a long-time member of the Fort Worth Club and when Clive first arrived there, Van took him under his wing, showing him the sights and introducing him to the members. Clive was very good-looking and I think Van was attracted to him, despite there being no doubt that Clive was heterosexual. At that time,

Van had a partner, Thomas Zaremba, a mortician. They later separated leading to an unpleasant court case when Thomas sued him for cash compensation but he lost.

I made many visits to Clive in Texas and I was introduced to Van. Often he would join me for lunch. During one visit, he invited me to a fantastic party he was giving in the club to celebrate his beloved mother's 90th birthday. He adored his mother and nothing was too good for her. Clive was given unlimited funds to put on the finest party possible. Singers from the Metropolitan Opera were brought from New York for a pre-supper show. A grand piano was hoisted in the elevator to the second floor and we all sat in gold chairs for a concert by members of the Metropolitan Opera, prior to the meal. Van played a special selection of his mother's favourites and then we adjourned to the dining room.

The room was decked out in the most beautiful display of flowers with enormous baskets of exotic blooms on the tables and flowers hanging in festoons from the ceiling. He had spent over $1,500 on the display. Specialist ice carvers had been hired to produce copies of famous buildings including the Kremlin, each one housing a large bottle of Russian vodka. The meal consisted of food from many countries and ranged from pâté de foie gras to enormous Texan fillet steaks; from Mexican specialities to Japanese tempura. The chefs had pulled out every stop. The wines were the finest and the toast was offered with the best of champagnes.

Van gave a great tribute to his mother whom he obviously adored and then he offered flowers to the guests to take home. He gave me an enormous basket of orchids. He later presented Clive with a cheque for $1,000 for him to buy something special as a thank you gift. On a later occasion, when he hosted a successful party for a Russian delegation, he sent me back to Britain with more flowers and thanked me for having such a wonderful son. From then on, my birthday flowers would always arrive. He was a tall man with a lot of curly hair, just beginning to go grey, always smiling and gracious – a truly remarkable and generous man.

'Fads don't interest me,' he is quoted as saying. He was renowned for having a predilection for suits and ties (both always navy), for old-fashioned chivalry and for fresh-cut flowers in his sprawling three-story Tudor mansion in Fort Worth. 'I belong to the 19th century, a time that celebrated beauty.'

Music Makers at Glyndebourne

My old friend Vernon Herbert had been caterer at Glyndebourne Opera for many years, first through Nuthalls Caterers, then with his own company. When John Christie's son George took over the management of Glyndebourne, I was asked to come in and review the catering operation, updating the meals offered to the cast, crew and other staff. This led to my involvement with the opera company in 1982 for a five-month period during which I met many of the most famous people in this colourful world. I was able to watch rehearsals and see the fabulous productions brought to life. The most memorable of these was *Orfeo and Euridice*, where the part of Orfeo was sung by Janet Baker in her very last operatic appearance. It was a demanding role and she would ask me to join her at the table during her lunchtime break from rehearsals, to prevent too many people interrupting her quiet time.

The conductor of this opera was Raymond Leppard and the producer, Peter Hall. Peter Hall was also producing *The Barber of Seville*, sung in Italian. His new wife Maria Ewing sung the role of Rosina in the second part of the season once she had given birth to their first child, Rebecca. It was obvious that Peter was besotted with Maria. When they lunched together, he was constantly embracing her. He required personal attention from us as caterers but as the days went by we became friends and I would sometimes join him for coffee as he relaxed. In those days he wore a fetching goatee beard and a small moustache. He was a very handsome man with the most piercing eyes. He was definitely attractive to women and fathered six children with his four wives.

It was a revelation to watch him, during the rehearsals, bringing out the very best from his cast. He seemed to have ultimate patience in coaxing the very last effort out of everyone to give a special polish to their performance. During this season he went on to produce a third successful performance of *Don Giovanni*.

The first production of the Festival at Glyndebourne was *The Love for Three Oranges*, produced by the American Frank Corsaro, a very friendly man who would often come and chat with me. He worked closely with Maurice Sendak who was the designer of this amusing opera, sung in French. His costume designs were delightful and capricious and he took a great part in the production. He died in May 2012 but his children's books will go on being read for a long time, especially *Where the Wild Things Are*. His obituary in the *New York Times* considered him the most important children's book artist of the twentieth century. The author Neil Gaiman described him as 'unique, grumpy, brilliant, gay, wise, and magical. He made the world better by creating art in it.'

I never found him grumpy, but instead a fascinating character. Once his work was done and the production on its way, he would spend a lot of time in the restaurant sketching. I got to know him very well and he wrote a delightful greeting and an original sketch for me in the special programme I still have, signed by so many of those great names present.

Reading the story of his life, I find he had an unhappy childhood. His parents were Jewish and he and his siblings were sent to the USA as children at the time of the Nazi purges, only to learn later that all their family had died in the camps. He said during an interview entitled 'Sendak on Sendak' at the Rosenbach Museum in Philadelphia, the place chosen as the repository for all his works:

'An illustrator in my own mind — and this is not a truth of any kind — is someone who so falls in love with writing that he wishes he had written it, and the closest he can get to is illustrating it. And the next thing you learn, you have to find something unique in this book, which perhaps even the author was not entirely aware of. And that's what you hold on to, and that's what you add to the pictures: a whole Other Story that you believe in, that you think is there.'

He was a very complex person and somehow I felt not a happy one, but he is someone I am proud of having met.

The singer who took the part of Le Roi in this production was another fascinating character, the bass-baritone Willard White. He was born in 1946 into a poor Jamaican family in Kingston, his father a dockworker and his mother a housewife. He learnt music by listening to the radio, especially singing Nat King Cole and Paul Robeson songs. By chance the wife of Sir John Barbirolli heard him sing and he was invited to study in London, but his father decided to buy him a ticket to New York 'because the flight was cheaper' and there he won a scholarship to study at the Juilliard School.

He has had an outstanding career, singing in many different roles but is also a talented actor and has starred as Othello with the Royal Shakespeare Company. In 2004 he was made a Knight Bachelor in the Queen's Birthday Honours. He was a very tall, outstanding figure and most gracious with us all. He would always ask, 'And how are you today?' and wrote on my programme, 'To a genuine person, from Willard White, thank you.'

Bernard Haitink was the principal conductor of the London Philharmonic Orchestra from 1967 to 1979 and they were the resident orchestra at Glyndebourne where Haitink was also the musical director from 1978 to 1988. He went on to receive many honours ranging from Honorary Companion of Honour to Honorary Knight Commander of the British Empire in Britain; the Order of the House of Orange for Arts and Science in his own country, the Netherlands, to a Grammy Award in the USA.

Raymond Leppard was a charming man with a great sense of humour. He had the most unusual laughing eyes and a deeply dimpled chin. His thick dark hair outlined a most interesting face. Born in England, he has appeared at concerts all round the world but he was a most approachable man and had a great rapport with the members of the orchestra. He was a regular customer in the lunch restaurant and always had a joke with the waitresses. I was able to attend many of the early rehearsals of *Orfeo and Euridice,* which he conducted, and marvelled at his ability to interpret the music in a most intense way for this most moving of operas.

Simon Rattle, then in his late thirties, was already making a name for himself. He was the conductor of *Der Rosenkavalier* and was a very serious young man, dedicated to his work. He had a mop of dark curly hair and was idolised by the waitresses. I would often see him wandering alone in the beautiful gardens of Glyndebourne in between rehearsals humming to himself but he would turn and give me a winning smile as he passed. He was the son of a naval officer and initially studied piano and violin but went on to become an orchestral percussionist. Only nineteen, he won the John Player competition for conducting and from then on his rise was explosive. Whilst at Glyndebourne, he was also the principal conductor and artistic adviser for the City of Birmingham Symphony Orchestra. Now knighted, he is recognised worldwide. It was great to see him in his early days when he was just making his way.

One of the joys of our stay at Glyndebourne, despite the challenge and the hard work involved, was having the chance to see these great musicians at work during rehearsal. It was an unforgettable experience.

It is noticeable that so many of these famous musicians, artists and singers seemed to have married several times. Perhaps it is a by-product of a life lived so close to their art.

Beau Younghusband

As soon as I met the Younghusband family, I learned about my father-in-law's elder brother Cyril who, at the end of the First World War, had arrived in Kenya on a soldier/settler scheme. He had served with the Cavalry with distinction, married a New Zealander, had three sons and initially embarked on a life as a garage proprietor at Nanyuki in the foothills of Mount Kenya. This family were an intrepid lot!

Beau, short for Beaumont was born in 1936 and the youngest of my husband's cousin's, would have the most interesting of lives. I would constantly get reports of his activities and was anxious to meet him but it would not be until 1954 when this happened. Since then, we have been good friends, and have met both here in the UK and in South Africa, during the time my son was working over there. I have found out what a fascinating life he has lived.

Beau told me how in 1940, the Italian army, having occupied Ethiopia were threatening the border towns of adjacent Kenya as it was the main staging post for the British Army's Abyssinian campaign to restore Haile Selassie and liberate his country. This meant his local primary school was moved to farm buildings a hundred miles away. Beau, then about to have his fourth birthday, and his brother John were sent to a boarding school. In fact, the nearest the Italians came to attacking was when one plane crash-landed at a small outpost called Isiolo, because the pilot was lost. By then Beau's father had rejoined the British Army and was in the Intelligence Corps in Nairobi, eventually taking charge of the numerous prisoner-of-war camps, housing the Italians captured after our troops landed in Sicily and mainland Italy. Meanwhile, his wife continued running to the garage as well as serving as a nurse in the casualty-clearing station in Nanyuki.

At the end of the war, the family sold the garage and bought a farm at Thompson Falls, sixty miles away. It covered 3000 acres, with beef and dairy cattle as well as various crops. Beau explained that, as his father was an ex-Cavalry officer, there were always plenty of horses and the boys rode from an early age, taking part in gymkhanas, polo matches and racing – definitely encouraging competitiveness and leadership. In addition they rented a further 5000 acres of grazing so the boys had plenty of wild Africa in which to ride and explore. When on holiday from boarding school, life was pretty idyllic for them; helping on the farm; driving the tractors; hunting; and fishing.

When an old shrapnel wound from the First World War began to cause his father problems, they sold up and bought a smaller acreage about twenty miles away. This was just as well because eighteen months later, in 1952, emergency was declared at the start of the Mau Mau

Uprising. It was fortunate that they had by then reduced their labour force since most of the men came from the Kikuyu tribe – the main participants in the uprising. Their own cook, who had been with the family since before Beau was born, was arrested for being an oath administrator, a high position in the Mau Mau. However, this shortage of help on the farm meant that all of the horses had to go.

Many of the families nearby were put at great risk. One close friend, a doctor, was betrayed by her cook whom she had treated for a life-threatening illness and whose life she had saved. He let the Mau Mau into her home and her husband was killed. She escaped with her life, although losing an eye. She managed to get into her car, collapsing over the wheel as she arrived at a police station with only the noise of her horn warning them of her dilemma. It was a dangerous time for many of the white Kenyan families.

During the emergency in 1953, Beau joined the Kenya Police Reserve, a full-time force. He was one of many who manned police posts on the forest edge between the Kikuyu Reserve and the Aberdare Forest, from which the Kikuyu were operating. A year later, he joined the Kenya Regiment and after a successful training period, he was seconded to the British Army for a two year short-service commission.

He saw service in Germany, the UK and then was returned to Kenya as his special knowledge of both the local language and the area where the Mau Mau were operating was invaluable. He spent an exciting time in many special operations there before further service in Malaya.

At the end of his two years, he joined the Royal East African Automobile Association as an inter-territorial patrol. When moved to Mombasa as the port officer, he met and married Diane. After another change of occupation, he went into the motor business and became heavily involved in motor sport. This is when I heard of his successes in the East African Safari Rally, reckoned to be the toughest in the world, with the Ford Motor works team.

He learnt to fly and was accepted initially by the RAF to train at Cranwell. Having received an unexpected legacy from his aunt, he realised he was now able to pay for a commercial training. He realised how much he enjoyed flying and this became his lifetime career. It would lead to many more adventures and a change of scene. Kenyan life was changing; independence was fast approaching. Kenyatta, having been jailed as Mau Mau leader, was now to become President. The British Government became so concerned about the future of the non-native citizens that they offered to buy them out in case they became a liability. But this would entail leaving the country. Beau realised that despite being well-regarded in the motor trade, without any formal qualifications he might find it hard to find work. With a professional pilot's licence, the problem would be solved.

He applied and received a British licence, initially becoming a charter pilot and flying instructor. After completing a thousand hours he joined East African Airways. As it became "Africanised" standards changed. Not prepared to accept this, he moved to South Africa and became a captain in a South African Airline. He says life was not easy in their first five years there as the salaries were low compared with BOAC.

However, things improved when, in 1975, he took a job with Rio Tinto Zinc as their chief pilot, flying a new executive jet up to their recently opened uranium mine in South West Africa, which later became Namibia. They bought a lovely house in Bryanston and life improved during the next three years, until political events once more took a hand in his life. With the coming independence of Namibia, the company was forced to sever its connection with South Africa. He was made redundant and was back on the job market, before being offered the position of chief pilot for Rank Xerox flying all over Europe, to Africa and occasionally to the States. Sensibly realising his flying days might soon come to an end, he also took management of the company car fleet. Ten years later he moved to BP as Chief Pilot and then Aviation Manager, with new aircraft and opportunities to fly all over the world including to the Soviet Union.

This lasted until 1993 when the Chairman was ousted and the

company wound up. His flying career finally came to an end after a spell with a Greek airline and later managing the aircraft of a Saudi Prince. He decided to retire and now lives in the peace and quiet of the Isle of Wight having travelled the world in high-powered jets. He has certainly added lustre to the Younghusband saga.

Alain Ouaiki and a Nose

Chris Pollard was approached by an international company, Julian Jill, to market perfumes in Britain as part of a multi-level marketing process. I was asked to work with him in this new venture. Initially I worked from my home in Wiltshire and from the outset it was very successful, making instant profit.

The owner, Alain Ouaiki, had an uncle working in the perfume industry who was known as a 'nose'. This is the name given to experts who are adept at identifying the flowers and aromas included in perfumes. He was able to decipher the formula for many of the most famous perfumes. The company would reproduce these perfumes, giving it a number and not a name, selling them by the multi-level method at a much lower price than the originals. He had based his business in France on the American Amway method. Amway, an abbreviation of the 'American Way' began as a detergent company but rapidly expanded.

He approached Chris Pollard with a view to creating a branch of his company Julian Jill in Britain. When it was set up, I was asked to become Managing Director. The French company enrolled the first two group sales leaders, recruiting them from the Amway sales force and they would then recruit others. Our job was to import stock and supply these sales people. We would also have to collect the money, pay the sales commissions and buy supplies from the production company in France. The venture started whilst we lived in Bratton. We had plenty of storage room and the company was very successful in its first year 1983. The growing sales force was invited to Marseille to visit the factory and enjoy a barbecue at the home of Monsieur Ouaiki so they would understand the product.

The board decided the following year to relocate to Wales. However, this unfortunately coincided with a year of turmoil, ending in the long miner's strike which crippled so many small businesses. Sales decreased, the sales team lost heart but expenses still had to be met as by then there was a warehouse and staff to pay. The first year's profits were being eaten up. Reluctantly we decided to close down the business. Alain Ouaiki was not pleased, especially when we returned all unsold stock to him. But more importantly Peter, my husband, was devastated because he knew how much effort we had put in to the venture. This would be one of the things that contributed to his heart attack and death in the following year. Research shows that the French branch is continuing to operate but for us it was a tragic ending to an initially good idea.

Peter Francis Younghusband – My Husband and My Closest Friend

When Peter and I married, we did not know each other at all. We had an instant physical attraction and I found him amusing; he said he found me interesting. It was wartime, we never thought further than the present because we did not know whether we would be alive tomorrow. After a short honeymoon perhaps we knew a little more about each other, I am not sure. Then within two months we were parted by my secret posting to Belgium. Many years later I found a letter he had written, addressed to no-one. In it he said, *'Why has she agreed to go on an overseas posting? Married women are not normally sent abroad. Is it that she does not love me? Does she know how much I love her?'* This sort of dilemma happened often in wartime but it was usually the man who was sent off on a special mission and not the woman.

My feelings were perhaps different; I knew the reason why I was being sent. Together with seven others, I had been selected for my ability to do swift mathematical calculations, in order to track the launch sites of the V2s. Was I more patriotic or more proud at having been chosen? I cannot say. But Peter, who was sensitive and tender-hearted, obviously suffered a great deal. I was to see him only for one night during the next eight months when I returned for twenty-four hours to collect a consignment of sports items to provide relaxation for the airwomen in Belgium. I would not return home again until late June 1945, six weeks after war had ended. Peter had by then completely finished the flat over the stables, working on his days off and preparing for my return.

We had never thought about what we would do when the war ended or talked about having children. Yet soon after returning home and long before I was demobbed I found I was pregnant. I told no one other than Peter as I realised that if I delayed my demobilisation, at least we would get my service pay for a longer period. Having made this decision, again we were parted for a period of three weeks whilst I was sent on a training course, 'Learning how to Teach'.

I began to think about how we would cope in a peacetime world with a child coming. We had until then, made no post-war plans. When I finally left the service in January 1946, I continued to teach Polish pilots from our flat until they, too, were demobbed. Our son was born just a week before Peter became a civilian once more. He found a post as a sales representative very quickly and was provided with a car. Since he had driven motorbikes since he was sixteen, he received a driving licence immediately – there was no such thing in those days as driving tests. We started our married life with Peter travelling every day over several counties and me filling my spare time doing the accounts and secretarial work for the riding school. I began to get to know the man I had married.

He was great at mending things, hated academic learning and was an amusing raconteur. He was loyal and obviously loved me and would do anything to help me. We worked for almost twenty-five years as a team, never falling out and each contributing what we were good at. Sometimes we worked over a hundred hours a week. Few couples work so closely together day upon day without disagreements – it was impossible to hide one's shortcoming from each other. Yet we survived. I hope it was a successful marriage. I have already realised that there is not just one person in this wide world with whom one can find happiness, but also I believe that having made a promise, one should do one's best to keep it.

Having moved frequently from hotel to hotel as managers and then succeeding in having our own business, we finally bought a lovely thatched house to escape to. We had worked hard and perhaps overworked. Peter had a breakdown and we decided to give up the hotel and work as freelance catering consultants, fitting in the hours to give us a little more leisure time. We moved to our house. Peter was happy to work in the garden, repair anything that needed it and indulge in his favourite pastimes of game fishing and rough shooting. He was a master at both having been brought up on the farm attached to the riding school.

On our return from our two years in America from 1972 to 1974, we continued with consultancy work and Peter had his first heart attack. It was totally unexpected although perhaps after his earlier breakdown, we should have been more aware. However, he seemed to recover successfully. We realised that the maintenance of our beautiful thatched house, because of its age, was becoming an increasing burden both from the expense but also the efforts Peter was putting in to maintain it. When I was invited to become director of Julian Jill, the perfume company, we reluctantly decide to sell up and move to Wales.

This move was to lead to his death. One day in April 1985, we returned home after a visit to friends in Cirencester. Peter was watching the still-remembered final of the snooker championship, between Steve Davis, the world champion, and the Northern Irishman, Dennis Taylor. It was at its crucial point, 11-11. I was suddenly conscious of Peter making strange noises in his throat – he appeared to be choking. Rushing to his side, I realised he was having a heart attack. I had no knowledge of what I should do but I did my best by trying to breath into his mouth. I thought he was responding when air seemed to come back out. I was desperate. I knew that the first four minutes were crucial.

Tragically it was the same day as the Welsh ambulance drivers strike so in desperation, between breaths, I rang my friends, the Pollards, and told them to get my doctor, a personal friend, to come at once. I returned to my efforts. All three friends arrived within fifteen minutes but it was too late. The doctor took one look and checked all vital signs. He turned to me, shaking his head and then he gave the thumbs-down sign – something which I will never forget. Peter, my husband and my loyal companion, was dead.

While visiting our friends in Cirencester that day, Peter had helped our friend, an ex-RAF Hercules pilot, move his dinghy to a new mooring. Was it this exertion which caused his death? We had returned home on the M4 and I often think that it might have happened on that motorway with disastrous consequences to other travellers on the road.

Peter had gone. We had been through so much together, good times and bad. I had not only lost my husband but a very special friend who had put up with me for more than forty years.

Going Solo

Jean Fernand – A Man from the Resistance

I found life very difficult to face after losing my husband so suddenly after forty years, having always worked so closely together, especially as my son was so far away. I realised that I had to do something to occupy and challenge myself so I decided to study. First I joined a French class and later went to Cardiff University's Lifelong Learning Department to improve my Spanish.

Soon after this a friend in the French class received, from a relative who had been in France throughout the war, a book entitled *J'y étais – I was there*. She asked if I could translate it for her as she spoke no French. My fellow French students decided we would take a chapter each.

The book tells the story of Jean Fernand and his colleagues during the Occupation. Monsieur Fernand was given the title of Honorary Mayor of the town of Apt having served as mayor in this community for over thirty years. During the war, he was one of first members of the famous Maquis resistance force who operated in the south of France in the wild territory there. This was how I learned of the sabotage work they had done in the region to hamper the occupying forces. His story intrigued me.

My brother had suggested I meet him in Paris and drive down to Cannes for a break. I realised we would be passing near the town of Apt so I wrote to Monsieur Fernand asking if I could meet him, and explaining we were intending to translate his book. He said he was honoured we would do this and he would let me have copies of the photos he had included in the French edition.

Apt lies north of Aix-en-Provence and the river Durance in the valley of the river Calavon and at the foot of the north-facing slopes of the Luberon Mountains. It is a picturesque town, famous for the production of crystallised fruits. Arriving at the house on the outskirts of the town, I walked through a beautiful garden. I still remember the mulberry tree in full bloom just outside the front door.

The door was opened by a man wearing a blazer bearing a military badge, and a smart shirt and tie. *'Entrez et bienvenue,'* he greeted me with a kiss on both cheeks and ushered me into a sitting room lined with bookshelves and memorabilia. It was obvious he was extremely organised. On the table were two glasses and a bottle of Vermouth. He invited me to sit down and then, pouring out two glasses, he said *'Santé et bienvenue!'* He lifted his glass and then handed me a copy of his book, signed and with my name and the inscription, *'Ces quelques souvenirs sur la Resistance au Pays d'Apt. Bien amicalement Juno.'* – 'Some memories of the Resistance in the district of Apt. With friendship, Juno.' This, I realised, must have been his wartime codename.

Over a welcome glass of Vermouth, he told me of some of his experiences. His team would lay out the landing flares when British planes brought in members of the SOE to help in the liaison with British Intelligence. These aircraft would be from squadrons based in North Africa and later Italy. Some of the SOE members were women who acted as radio operators. Amongst them was a Polish countess who had flown in on several occasions. As he remembered her, tears came into his eyes. He described how, on many occasions, he had hidden her in his home. Her name was Countess Maria Krystyna Skarbek. She was beautiful, brave and reckless and had many lovers. I suspect Jean Fernand may have been amongst them. The work she did for the SOE earned her the reputation that her courage and audacity had no equal.

Jean Fernand said he had hidden many escaping airmen as they were being escorted to freedom over the border into Italy or Spain. He described vividly how during a British raid on a German army camp nearby, one of the Wellington bombers had been hit and the aircraft crashed in his area. His team of Maquis managed to locate it in a ravine. He described the scene in horrific detail. Only one of the crew had managed to get out but his parachute had failed to open and his body was found nearby partially burnt by the exploding ammunition. They removed all his papers. The rest of the crew had been consumed by the flames, and only charred remains were left.

The Maquis secretly buried them. He described it to me, 'This intimate ceremony was very poignant, my friend the poet René Char, alias Alexandre, read the funeral service.' At the end of hostilities their remains were reinterred and they now lie in the British Military Cemetery in Marseille. Very soon after the tragedy, all the name tags and the papers they could retrieve were returned to London. The remainder of the plane was swiftly secreted away and all instruments hidden. The Germans never knew what had happened.

Jean Fernand had many stories of the Resistance. I was invited to visit his personal museum in his garage to see his collection of papers and memorabilia of the work done by the Maquisards during those dire days. The town of Apt was awarded membership of the Legion d'Honneur for its contribution in the Resistance and Jean Fernand was made an Officer of the Legion d'Honneur, as well as receiving the King's Medal from George VI, the Croix de Guerre and the American Medal of Freedom. He was a very brave and honourable man.

Douglas Hurd

In 1989 Chris Pollard became High Sheriff for the county of South Glamorgan and I had the privilege of attending several events with him. On one occasion, he and his wife Vivien were invited, together with many Cardiff businessmen, to lunch at the House of Commons. On this occasion his wife was unable to attend so Chris invited me to take her place. Several MPs joined us for lunch but the one I especially remember is Douglas Hurd. I sat next to him throughout the meal and had a long and interesting conversation with him. He served both under Margaret Thatcher and John Major in various ministerial positions but was perhaps most remembered as a successful Foreign Minister.

During lunch, he related to me all the meetings he had already had that day and those he had to attend during the rest of the day. The total amounted to over twenty, culminating with one with the Prime Minister, Margaret Thatcher, that evening. He was obviously a dedicated politician but also was a very entertaining luncheon companion, and despite the feelings we all have about politicians at the moment, someone I felt I could trust implicitly, who served his country with distinction.

Lord Longford and Lord Lyell

My next experience, also through Chris Pollard, was luncheon in the House of Lords at the invitation of the Welsh member, Lord Parry of Neyland, then head of the Welsh Tourist Board. On arrival we were allocated to different tables, each with one or two Welsh Peers present. We were warned not to mention Myra Hindley if we were seated at the table with Lord Longford. Guess who was allocated a seat bang opposite the said Lord? Yes, I was! After we all had introduced ourselves to him and the other Peer present, Lord Lyell, we started a polite conversation. To our surprise, Lord Longford broke in immediately, bringing up Myra Hindley and asking our opinion on whether she should be released.

It seems she was still in love with Brady and tried to get Frank Longford to arrange a meeting between them. Of course this would not be permitted but Longford persisted in believing she was a reformed character. I think she used him, but eventually found the association did her case for early release more harm than good and referred to him as 'a pestilential pain'.

I am sure he believed she was a reformed character to the end. However, I would have preferred a slightly more savoury subject for the lunchtime discussion. The gentleman on my right, Lord Lyell, was a far more charming and pleasant man. When he learned that my granddaughter lived in America, he said she should learn more about the land of her father and after lunch, took me down to a shop in the entrance to the Lords, where they sold memorabilia. He insisted on buying me books and brochures on London landmarks such as Big Ben and the Tower of London, and he wrote a message to her, telling her about Parliament and then signing it. I thought that was a lovely gesture and of course thanked him for his kindness.

I was delighted to learn that he was one of the ninety-two elected hereditary peers to remain in the House of Lords, after the House of Lords Act in 1999 when hereditary peers lost their automatic right to sit in the House of Lords.

Jeffrey Archer and George Thomas

Once again through Chris Pollard's contacts, I briefly met Jeffrey Archer at a social function at the Pollard's home. He was charismatic and appeared sincere in his beliefs. He spoke well which is always an asset to a politician. However, there was one great figure in Welsh politics whom I had the pleasure of meeting on just one occasion and there was absolutely no doubt in my mind of his sincerity. That was the man who carried out his duties as Speaker of the House with such acclaim, George Thomas, a man from the Valleys who was a near neighbour of the Chairman of the Parish Council in my Wiltshire village of Bratton. George Thomas showed how, despite one's background, it is possible to arrive at greatness.

John Gilbert

At a private dinner party in the Pollard's house in Kensington I met another eminent parliamentarian, John Gilbert, who later became Life Peer, Baron Gilbert and Privy Councillor. He attended with his wife whose company in the Virgin Islands was negotiating the purchase of the Pollard's property. He was an interesting conversationalist. At one stage I asked him why he supported the Labour party: 'That's easy to answer. While I was at Oxford, I was looking for a part-time job to supplement my income and I saw that the Labour Party was asking for help during their pre-election campaign. I applied and was given the job of stuffing the envelopes with their propaganda leaflets. I could see that I could improve their organisation and make my mark so I decided to join the Party.' He proved his point and by 1960 was elected as the MP for Dudley and later for Dudley North where he served until 1990. Then retiring from Parliament he became Baron Gilbert, Privy Councillor. He came from an affluent background, having been educated at Merchant Taylors' School, Northwood, and St John's College, Oxford, as well as New York University.

Sir Peter Webster

Part of the duties of High Sheriff, a tradition harking back to Saxon times, was to ensure the welfare of visiting High Court judges, to attend on them at court and to offer them hospitality. It was customary to invite people of the area who were knowledgeable and influential to the welcoming dinner. The guests were requested to arrive in advance of the visiting judge and not leave before him. They were introduced and instructed to wait to speak until spoken to – obviously a very formal occasion. I was very privileged to be invited to these dinners on several occasions during Chris Pollard's year of office and, being a newcomer to South Glamorgan, I was not known by many of the invited guests. I think some of them wondered why I was there.

On the very first of these judicial visits, we awaited the arrival of the guests of honour. I had not been told the name of the judge and his wife and was awaiting their appearance with interest. Imagine my surprise when as they glanced around the room, they both shouted, 'Hello Eileen, fancy meeting you here!' It was Sir Peter Webster and his wife April who I had met in Bratton, the village where until very recently we had owned the Duke Hotel. It was through us that they had found their house there.

Arranging to stay a weekend at our hotel, they mentioned on arrival they were looking for a house to buy in the area. The mother of a friend of mine had recently died and her daughter was looking for a buyer for her beautiful thatched cottage in the village. Effecting an introduction between the interested parties, a deal was arranged within those few days and not only did they buy the house but also all the antique furniture in it as well. The whole matter was settled without the need of an estate agent, saving the fees in the bargain. The Websters had since become firm friends.

Peter Webster was an imposing figure and one of the most sought-after barristers of his time. Three years younger than I was, he had spent the last two years of the war as a Fleet Air Arm pilot, protecting merchant shipping and flying Corsairs from aircraft carriers in the Indian Ocean.

I was privileged to attend several more of these evenings with visiting judges and found most of them both charming and interesting. Fortunately I have only met judges in such friendly surroundings!

George Comes Back Into My Life…

Having adjusted to life alone, I made every effort to renew old contacts, make new ones and join stimulating classes. It was in the summer of 1998 that my old school in Southgate notified me of a reunion for scholars who had attended when it was still a grammar school, prior to its conversion to a comprehensive. I decided to attend and persuaded my brother to include the date in a proposed visit. I telephoned many of my old companions to make sure they were coming and managed to obtain the phone number of my first love. George was now living near Newcastle, I learned, with his wife and an unmarried daughter, his sole offspring. I decided to phone him in the hope he might also manage to attend the reunion. He answered the phone and my heart leapt as I recognised his soft slightly Scottish accent. He was obviously very surprised to hear me but said it was impossible for him to get away to the reunion, without explaining why. He asked for my phone number and said he would call me back, speaking very quietly as if he did not wish to be overheard. I rang off and wondered if I would ever hear from him again.

It would not be until nearly three years later that I would receive that phone call. Then he talked openly, explaining life had been difficult. He spent most of his time with his Masonic Lodge activities, his membership of the Royal Military Police Association and other male activities. He told me his daughter was suffering from an illness which turned out to be a form of cancer. I asked him why all those years ago, he had not written to me himself and told me about his marriage. He told me that he had been ashamed. I did not know then how to interpret that answer. He explained it was difficult to phone but at the moment the house was empty. I read from that he did not want his conversation to be heard. He added, 'I have become a misogynist!'

He promised to send me some photographs and they arrived by return of post. They showed a beautiful garden and a large number of uniformed officers present at a reunion he gave each year for Dunkirk veterans. There was also a picture of him with his wife in a wheelchair and their daughter, a very beautiful-looking girl. There was a further photo of him outside the Tower of London with a uniformed companion and a civilian friend.

It was difficult to read the situation. He told me he was hoping to travel to a reunion in Berlin where he had served post-war in the Military Police and that he might also be coming to a rugby match in Cardiff when he would come and visit me. From then onwards, he rang me once a month. On a later occasion he explained that his wife had had a massive stroke and needed a mechanical hoist night and morning to get her in and out of her wheelchair. He added that he had moved back into her bedroom after many years in separate rooms, to care for her during the night since her carers only came during the day. There seemed to be a lot more behind what he was saying but, above all, I could see that he was a caring man.

In June 2006, he had said he was going into hospital for tests and a month later said the problem had been resolved. On 16th December I received his last phone call, assuring me he would ring over Christmas. That call never came. I sent a card for his birthday on 3rd February signed only E, but again heard nothing. By March I was worried and I decided to write him a letter asking if everything was alright. Some weeks later after no news, wishing to put my worries to rest, I finally decided to phone. An unknown male voice answered, 'This is Gwyn answering the phone as Jean Duncan is in hospital.' I paused for a moment, surprised, before asking if I could speak with Mr George Duncan. There was a long pause, 'I am sorry to tell you he died on the morning of Hogmanay.'

I was shocked but felt I had to explain why I was calling in case the letter I had sent had caused a problem. I learned then that George had been taken ill on the day before Christmas Eve and had died a week later. I was given the phone number of a very close friend of George so I could learn more.

The tragedy was that after caring for both his wife and daughter for many months and perhaps years, he was the one who had died. I spoke to his daughter later when she returned from hospital as I felt sure she had probably opened my letter, to explain I was an old school friend of George's. She told me that her mother was now in a home. It was only a few months later that I learned that they had both died within a year of George. For me it is an unfinished story.

Major Bill Fussell of The Royal Artillery – Here Comes The Army!

About eighteen months after my husband died, I received a phone call from one of the Territorial officers who had been at camp in north Devon and later had been a frequent visitor with his mother to the West Country Inn during our time there. He was sending his belated condolences on losing Peter but added something which bewildered me: 'You know, if I had not done what I did do, and done what I had intended, you would have left your husband.'

I had remembered him as one of a pleasant group of officers from a Reading Territorial unit. The name had stuck with me as someone at school had the same name and was, I believe, a distant relative, but I could not remember what he looked like. He went on to say, 'Do you remember you were invited by our regiment to come and view the Lord Mayor's Show and you were a guest for the night at the Colonel's house?' I thought back and vaguely remembered that we had all returned for a reunion dinner at the house where I was staying but that was about all I could recall.

He went on, 'After everyone went to bed, I came to your bedroom – and then changed my mind and left.' I was completely confused by now and tried to think back all those years to 1960. I had a dim recollection of being almost asleep after a hectic evening, then being aware of the door opening and a figure approaching the bed. Before I could call out, the figure turned and retreated and the door shut again. At the time, I dismissed it as one of the guests, after perhaps a little too much wine, coming to the wrong room, realising his mistake and beating a hasty retreat. Now it seemed it had been more than that – he had come with evil intent!

I was highly amused and wondered why he was telling me this now but said nothing. Anyhow he said he was on his way to north Wales to visit a lady friend and asked if could he call in and see me. I agreed and this started a rather strange relationship. Initially he was amusing and friendly, often staying for a night on his way north to see this lady. Occasionally it would be a couple of nights and we would go out to dinner or take a drive to the Gower Peninsula which, I learned, was where he had spent a lot of time during the war with the Royal Artillery. He would travel with the Air Observation Post Squadrons in Auster aircraft checking the accuracy of artillery fire against enemy aircraft.

After several visits, his attitude changed and he tried to get a little more 'friendly'. He was an interesting companion as far as I was concerned but nothing more and frankly no oil painting. The end to a beautiful friendship came when he wrote advising me of his next visit and adding, 'There is no need for separate rooms this time.' I made it clear that was not what I was interested in and hoped he would respect that. He was persistent and so it ended with my no longer being available for bed and breakfast.

I saw him one further time when staying with friends at Sandbanks, Poole, near to where he had a flat. I met him for lunch, accompanied by another friend. But I always received a birthday card signed – Love from Bill – until a couple of years ago. I assume he is now elsewhere. I always thought it a little presumptuous to think that all those years ago I would have been so enamoured of him to break up my family.

Lieutenant Colonel Simon West Introduces Raymond Baxter

Around the year 2000, the BBC invited everyone with an interesting Second World War story to send it to them to create an archive of interesting events. I sent a copy of an article I had written about the Filter Room and the importance of Radar in the defence of Britain as well as information on V1 and V2 detection. This resulted in a contact which has led to much that has followed in recent years. Lieutenant Colonel Simon West of the Royal Artillery found the article and read it.

He was based at the Defence Academy at Shrivenham in Wiltshire as one of the lecturing team. Courses were run on many military subjects, for all services and officers of varying ranks. He was preparing for a series of talks on the various uses of Radar to a group of four hundred Majors on a three-month course. He knew nothing about the Filter Room at the time and decided to contact me. He visited my house and made a short video of my reminiscences and told me on leaving he was going on to meet Raymond Baxter. This well-known broadcaster served in the RAF as a Spitfire pilot. One of his assignments was to destroy the launching sites of the V1 rockets sited in the Pas-de-Calais area of France.

I was invited to join Raymond at Shrivenham to hear his presentation. We sat in the front row of a large lecture hall, filled with military students in rank after rank of seating, rising to the ceiling. I sat on the right-hand side of the Brigadier General whom we had met the night before at dinner.

After the introduction, the video interviews of Raymond and I were shown, followed by a film. Imagine my surprise when I appeared on the screen, in WAAF Officer's uniform, aged about twenty. I grabbed the Brigadier's arm and, in total amazement, said 'I cannot believe it – that's me!' I remembered that a film company, Nettlefold Studios, had filmed events at Fighter Command Filter Room during an evening watch in November 1943. They had filmed three different sessions in order to choose the one where most events such as hostile raids, interceptions, and bombing activities took place. It was not designed for public consumption but for the use of the scientific observers and RAF Radar specialists, to see whether they could learn from it. I recalled the name of the film director – Blaydon Peake – because he had taken me out to dinner after one of the sessions. And here was I, all those years later, looking at the finished creation, one in which I appeared filtering the track of a hostile aircraft.

After the initial interview with me, Simon West had contacted the Imperial War Museum for anything they had on the Filter Room, and this film was found in their archives. He kindly sent a copy to me and then I applied for the right to use it if I should give talks on the subject, little realising then where it would lead.

Raymond kept in touch by phone after we returned. He was a lovely person – so open and unaffected by fame. I made a second visit to Shrivenham some months later when it had been hoped he would join us. Sadly he had already arranged, despite appalling weather, to give the commentary at the Goodwood Festival of Speed, Goodwood Circuit. This lead to an illness from which he died.

Since that first meeting, I have had frequent contact with Simon West whose military life since those days has lead him to working with the Territorial Army and a long stint in Afghanistan, and later a stay in the United States in a diplomatic capacity. Now he has returned to Shrivenham. I look on him as the stimulant which led me on to write my first book, the beginning of a very active life for a 'has been'.

The Icing on the Cake

Carlos Mingo

Before we moved into the twenty-first century, I decided to keep my brain active and found that the facilities available at Cardiff University's Centre for Lifelong Learning were phenomenal. My enrolment there led to my meeting many interesting lecturers as well as, late in life, having the opportunity to acquire the Diploma of Higher Education in Spanish Grammar, Literature and History and Creative Writing; equivalent to the first two years towards a Bachelor's degree. Always having regretted the loss of a university education, I took advantage of this and in the first year that it was awarded, I was one of the first five students to receive the diploma.

The lecturer for one of my elected subjects was Carlos Mingo, a young and inspiring Spanish teacher. He was brought up in the province of Valladolid and obtained his first degree in Literary Theory and Criticism, later writing his Master's dissertation on modern Arthurian literature. Recently he gained his Doctorate for his dissertation on the trilogy *The Warlord Chronicles* by Bernard Cornwell. Carlos had a joint heritage of Romanian and Spanish ancestry and is bilingual. His lectures were stimulating and demanding; he would not let his students get away with second best. My life has certainly been enriched by knowing him and learning from him. He has been teaching Spanish since 1998, initially in a secondary school. Due to his great ability he is now teaching undergraduates and postgraduates in Cardiff University but continues his connection with older students, teaching interesting courses in Spanish Literature, History and Cinema. He has many publications ranging from articles entitled 'Women, Politics, Religion: the Reshaping of Arthuriana' to medical and pharmaceutical translations and case studies.

John Greeves – Poet and Teacher

One of the most helpful lecturers in Creative Writing, whose classes were always enjoyable, was John Greeves. He managed to bring back memories and instil in us the confidence to write. His input during these sessions helped me considerably when I went on to write my autobiography *Not an Ordinary Life*. His preparation for the class was impressive and I for one came away feeling ready to pick up my pen and create a masterpiece.

As well as a teacher, John is a poet, short-story and feature writer. He has taught at Cardiff Centre for Lifelong Learning for the past six years. John believes in the power of poetry to change people's lives, but feels it is important to make poetry accessible in a language which moves and connects to the modern world. He believes everyone has a story to tell, and that it is important in the process of writing to encourage others in a supportive and positive way. The BBC broadcast one of his stories called *Ties*, which appeared as a segment feature programme. He has recently published *Cuba Libre: from Revolution to Hip-Hop-Rock*, a collection of poems taking the reader on a journey through Cuban life. It encompasses the iconic images of the island, revealing the lasting beauty of the 'land of miracles'.

Paul Traynor – Journalist and Trekker

One further person honed my skills in a specialised form of writing – journalism. I spent ten weeks under the guidance of Paul Traynor but the value of this course was immense. Journalistic writing is quite different from any writing I had previously undertaken. One of his great pieces of wisdom was to remind us of the short attention span of most readers of newspapers and to make certain that all the vital pieces of information appeared at the beginning of a report since interest tailed off if articles were too long. He had a wealth of experience on regional and national newspapers.

Graduating in Economics from Cardiff University in 1975, aged twenty he worked as a labourer at British Dredging Ltd on Newport docks and spent a couple of years as a steelworker before becoming a civil servant. His real passion was mountain walking, carrying only a tent, food and gear for a few days at a time. This led to an offer from a travel writer to accompany him on a backpacking trip to the eastern Pyrenees. Since it was taking place early in the year, in dangerous snowy conditions at altitude, he needed a companion. Despite a few risky moments, it all went well and several more trips followed. His companion was the late Rob Neillands, an ex-Royal Marine Commando who went on to become a respected military historian. Paul was gaining varied experiences to draw on for his journalism in the future.

This contact led to a post with Haymarket Publishing as a trainee editor for an outdoor magazine. Within a month his first feature article was published and he continued his journalistic education in-house and on block release at the London School of Printing. His backpacking and mountain-walking experiences took him, over many years, to places ranging from the Swiss Jura Ridgeway, the Tour du Mont Blanc, the Pyrenean High Route from the Atlantic to the Mediterranean, the Corsican High Level Route, the Italian Apennines, the Auvergne and the Pennine Way closer to home. In addition he was freelancing as a writer and a part-time sub-editor on local daily newspapers in South Wales and later for the *Sunday Express*.

Taking voluntary redundancy from two newspapers within three years, he now continues editing a Government website. He reports that the walking has become less adventurous with gammy knees from hiking with a heavy pack and a few years as rugby prop forward but he is planning a few more mountain trips and working on a website encouraging minimal impact good practice in the great outdoors.

He started teaching 'Non-Fiction Writing for Newspapers and Magazines' as an evening course in the mid-1990s. He says like so many freelance writers he needed to supplement his income. Nearly sixty people turned up for the first class and he found he enjoyed the interaction with the students.

Dr Ian Spring – Senior Lecturer in the Department of Creative Writing

Probably the lecturer who had the greatest effect on my writing was Dr Ian Spring. He was, at the time, head of the Literature Department of Lifelong Learning and had instigated a course entitled Publishing. This course was taught on a one-to-one basis online. Its second year on the schedule coincided with the time when I was writing my autobiography *Not an Ordinary Life*. Since I was fairly well-known in the department, he offered to conduct it on a face-to-face basis. I would work each week with him in his study at the University and I was instructed to finish the remaining chapters before Christmas.

Starting in September, I transferred the completed part of my script on to a memory stick. Then using the Adobe Indesign programme, we transferred it on to the computer screen. Working from there we then chose the font, the spacing, the layout and the headings. As we progressed, we chose appropriate photos for insertion to which I then added captions. It was a fascinating process. Dr Spring had a great aptitude for design and he produced the cover layout. We then sent out draft copies for reviews and inserted them. I compiled the index and it was almost ready to go. I found a printer and the Lifelong Learning department were so pleased with the result that they allowed it to be published under their name. It was a great thrill to receive the first proof copies. A launch date was decided upon and over one hundred people attended. Dr Spring had brought to life my first published book. To my surprise, I was notified recently that Ian had been instrumental in recommending me for an award in the Queen's New Year's Honours List for assisting in the campaign to prevent the Humanities department of the Cardiff University Learn section being axed. This resulted in a British Empire Medal. I am both honoured and grateful.

The Chinese Connection – Professor Li Angui and the Seven Strangers

Spanish study at Cardiff University's Lifelong Learning Centre often involved practice in their Language Laboratory. On one occasion, there was a new overseas student present. He appeared to be oriental and was obviously having difficulty concentrating against a background of spoken Spanish. At the end of the lesson, I apologised for disturbing him. He was a man in his late forties who thanked me, saying 'I try to practise my English.' I asked him if he had had the opportunity to meet native speakers for this purpose. He replied, 'I do not know any but I practise with a Japanese friend.' Horrified I offered to help and invited him to my house reassuring him that I would not charge for this service. Angui was spending a year at the University in the Department of Architecture. He was a specialist in Build, the process of installing modern devices for heating, ventilation, sound-proofing etcetera. He began to visit each Saturday. His knowledge of the language was considerable but his accent appalling. He was involved in a joint study with the Department of Architecture and he would give me the papers he wrote for correction, always expressing his gratitude.

One Saturday he arrived with a bowl of dough for making a special Chinese delicacy. It made about one hundred little dumplings which I was encouraged to taste. What remained was then put in my freezer and they lasted for a year. He told me he was only allowed to bring about £3,000 with him in currency and this had to cover all his expenses for the year. We became great friends and I looked forward to our Saturday rendezvous. After a year he returned to his home town in the east of China but returned a year later for a further six months. This time he was allowed to bring his wife and young son for a three-month stay. Before they arrived he wrote and asked if I could arrange a school for his son to attend and I managed to get him into a central Cardiff comprehensive. I offered to accommodate them for the first two weeks since his wife would only arrive later for part of the stay.

It was most interesting to meet his son who knew nothing of Western ways. I first had to teach him how to use a knife and fork and some essential words in order to cope at school. The first word I taught him was 'toilet'. It was a great experience for me too – learning the difference in outlook and behaviour of a country so different from ours. When the family were reunited and took a flat in Cardiff, I was invited to Sunday lunch. Since they came from the east of China, the food was quite different from anything served in either Canton or Mandarin cooking. They were a delightful family and as a token of their thanks, on their return sent me a most beautiful book of cut-paper pictures, a special Chinese art.

Within the next year I would have another Chinese adventure. While having dinner with friends, the doorbell rang quite late in the evening. My host stepped into the lobby to open the door. We could hear him talking to at least two people. It was a young Chinese couple. They explained they were spending a year at Leeds University and were making their way to the Gower Peninsula. Realising they were not likely to get there in time to find a suitable B&B for the night, they had seen the lights on in this house and as it was in the middle of a county town, among the shops, had assumed it was an hotel! We laughed since we were all ex-hoteliers in the past.

My friend phoned several local bed-and-breakfast venues in the area, but none had accommodation available. In a moment of rash charity I offered them a bed for the night if they would follow me home. They accepted with alacrity but said, 'There are seven of us!' I felt having got so far I could do nothing but offer to put them all up!

There were two car loads and I insisted the young woman travel with me to act as a liaison. So off we went. We arrived at my house by 10.50 that evening. I had three spare rooms – there was the young couple, a husband and wife and a small boy and three individual men. By putting a mattress on the floor in two rooms, I managed to find a space for them all and since I have two bathrooms, I thought I could cope.

After they had sorted out where they were going to sleep, they asked if they could prepare some supper so after eleven o'clock, we started. They had everything with them, a container of soup, some stir-fry chicken and some dumplings. They insisted I join them for another meal. It was quite an occasion. They were all academics, a couple of professors and the rest M.A.s, all from different disciplines and from different parts of China. During the journey home I had been talking to the young woman and I had asked her whether they had had any difficulties with the students in Leeds and she admitted they had initially but did not understand why. I explained about the widespread knowledge here of the massacres of students in Tiananmen Square some years back. She said she had never heard about it and explained the area where she and her husband lived was near the Russian border and news from Beijing was scarce. She asked me if I would tell the others later about this.

During our supper together, I remembered this request and told them about the reports we had of the killing field in Beijing. They all seemed unaware of it and then the senior member of the group, Jyang Jun, who announced himself as a Professor of the Beijing Institute of Civil Engineering and Architecture, took the floor. He vehemently denied any such thing had happened and launched into a tirade against the Western press, warning his colleagues it was all lies. It was then I remembered that most groups of Chinese when visiting abroad were accompanied by a member of the Government, making certain they did not get contaminated by Western ideas. I tactfully changed the subject and said no doubt someone had got it wrong and we finished the meal amicably.

The next morning they all wrote in my visitor's book and I saw they were a very mixed group. The young family came from Yunnan where the husband was a computer specialist. The first couple I met came from Heilongjiang University where he was Director of the Foreign Students'

Office and she was a teacher of English. The most charming message left in my book was from Zhiming Wang from Shandong University. He wrote 'Confucius said - All the people in the world are brothers. I'm from Con's home town and so lucky to meet you. You are so kind, clever English lady. It worth me to remember all my life!'

This alone made up for all the work in washing seven loads of bed linen the following morning. I still occasionally hear from the young couple and more rarely from Zhiming Wang but I am so glad I was able to do something to further international relations.

Colin Dexter – The Creator of Morse

A few years ago, a series of weekend courses were offered in Creative Writing with various tutors covering different aspects of the craft, each weekend hosted by a well-known author. It was held in the beautiful surroundings of Duffryn Gardens in the Vale of Glamorgan, South Wales. I attended on three separate occasions. On the first occasion the author was Monica Dickens. The second occasion was attended by Colin Dexter, whose *Inspector Morse* books were at the height of their popularity as his iconic detective series Morse was broadcast. It soon became clear that the author and his cantankerous detective shared some idiosyncrasies. The evening following his opening speech to us all, we adjourned to the bar. He was sitting on his own when I entered. He beckoned me to join him but I had barely got my bottom on the seat when he turned to me and said, as imperiously as Morse would treat his minion Lewis, 'Get me a pint of bitter'. I laughed and thought at least it was memorable.

The subsequent conversation with him made up for the cost of the beverage; he was genuinely interested in what I enjoyed writing and asked some quite pertinent and sometimes amusing questions. I had nearly an hour of his personal time and felt highly honoured.

It was during a holiday in Wales, that he started writing mysteries, and the first Morse episode saw the light of day. He reports, 'We were in a little guesthouse, halfway between Caernarfon and Pwllheli. It was a Saturday and it was raining – it's not unknown for it to rain in north Wales. The children were moaning ... I was sitting at the kitchen table with nothing else to do, and I wrote the first few paragraphs of a potential detective novel.' *Last Bus to Woodstock* was published in 1975 and introduced the world to the character of Inspector Morse, the irascible detective whose penchants for cryptic crosswords, English literature, cask ale and Wagner reflected some of Dexter's own enthusiasms.

He has been the recipient of many honours during his career, including being appointed an Officer of the Order of the British Empire for services to literature and a year ago, the University of Lincoln awarded Dexter an Honorary Doctor of Letters degree.

Colin Dexter continues to make cameo appearances in the new series of *Lewis* as was his wont in Morse. He is now eighty-two-years-old, ten years younger than I am. I hope he is still enjoying his glass of draught beer and I would buy him another one tomorrow if he passed my way again.

Willie Robertson – On the Milk

It would be at a subsequent weekend course at Duffryn that we would meet Willie Robertson who had just written his amusing book *On the Milk*. This hilarious memoir evokes Willie Robertson's first working days as a delivery boy on the back of the local dairy's milk delivery van. It traces his efforts until he attains the ultimate – a journeyman deliverer when a teenager, embracing the exciting world of mods and rockers. It is set in Dundee in the early 1960s and it is evocative of the lives of many working-class teenagers of that time.

This tall languid writer was beguiling and constantly had us laughing. He went on to tell us of his next idea for a book and related how it had come to him whilst on a platform at a railway station. The story sounded as if it was almost complete and ever since I have been looking for it in print without success.

Hugh Turnbull – BBC Radio Wales

I find it comforting to think that in my eighties and now my nineties, I am still meeting interesting men. Most of these opportunities have sprung from my decision to write about my somewhat unusual life. This has led to radio and TV experiences and the opportunity to have my books published by an up-and-coming company in Cardiff. It began when I became involved in the campaign to fight the closure of many of the classes offered by the Humanities section of the Lifelong Learning Department of Cardiff University.

Citing cost-cutting as the reason, classes offering a lifeline to older citizens to continue learning and the opportunity to meet like-minded fellow students were scheduled to be removed. Having relied on these classes myself and knowing the benefits I had derived from them, including the chance finally to obtain a BA degree at the age of eighty-seven, I gave the campaign my full support. BBC Wales sent one of their producers to interview me. This is how I became acquainted with Hugh Turnbull, now a valued friend who comes to my rescue whenever modern technology gets beyond my capabilities. After our first meeting, when we discussed my wartime experiences, he returned to his producer and said, 'I think there is another programme there!'

This led to a further interview with Hugh and many other interviews and broadcasts for me. Hugh is one of the kindest people I have met in my life. We share an interest and love of wine although we are opposite in our political views. However, since all his family are of the same mind as himself and he enjoys a good argument, we allow ourselves what we call a frank discussion on the political events of the day when we meet. I enjoy this as much as I hope he does but there is no way that either of us is likely to change our beliefs.

Hugh was born in Luton where he started his career as a junior reporter with the *Luton News*. He worked for several other weekly newspapers, and spent a year as press officer for Bedfordshire County Council. He moved to Wales in 1975, joining the *Western Telegraph* at Haverfordwest. He reported on the spate of UFO sightings known as the 'Broadhaven Triangle'. Interestingly, I learned this fact on the day the Ministry of Defence issued an announcement that despite having checked on all reports of UFOs, they could assure us that there was no chance of us experiencing their landing on Britain.

In 1979 Hugh moved into radio reporting, initially with Swansea Sound and he remained true to this medium until his retirement in 2010. He became head of news at Swansea and won two Welsh Radio Journalist of the Year Awards, the first time it had been awarded to a commercial station. Ten years later, he joined the BBC in Cardiff where he produced numerous news programmes for BBC Radio Wales. He was nominated for a Sony Award in 2003 for a documentary about the Cwmaman Institute Silver Band reaching the final of the British Open Championships. I consider myself honoured that he decided to turn my story into a programme entitled 'My Secret War', which was aired three times on BBC Radio Wales.

Hugh retired in 2010 and I have had the pleasure and privilege of his support and friendship since. He has a mind which manages to eliminate the unnecessary and focus on the important and he certainly keeps me on my toes. Through his encouragement, I wrote my second book and have even made an occasional appearance on the 'box'!

Roy Noble – A Mainstay of Afternoon Radio

Since fronting a campaign to make the drug Lucentis available in Wales on the NHS, I have been interviewed on several occasions by BBC Radio Wales. I was getting used to being questioned on the morning news programme but it was a total surprise to receive an invitation to appear on the popular weekday afternoon show hosted by Roy Noble. A taxi picked me up and I was taken first into the recording studio and saw the programme in action. Through the glass window I could see and hear Roy interviewing his first guest.

I had to admit that as I never put the radio on in the daytime, I had no idea of his technique. He seemed to have quite a regional accent but I was to find later that this could change according to whom he was speaking. I quickly saw his ability to draw out his interviewee and I began to relax. I thoroughly enjoyed the experience as we discussed the recent launching of *One Woman's War* on my ninetieth birthday at RAF St Athan. I have since done a further two interviews with him, one just prior to Christmas when I shared the occasion with a nurse who had now become a missionary and three lovely young girls singing Christmas carols, as well as Captain Sir Norman Lloyd-Edwards, a former Cardiff Lord Mayor.

Roy Noble's first professional career was in education and he held several positions throughout Wales as headmaster. He gradually moved over to broadcasting having written and presented a weekly letter from Aberdare. His afternoon programme has attained some of the highest listening figures in Wales and he is a much loved and respected broadcaster. Appearing on his show was quite an adventure as I had no idea what he was going to ask me. He now has altered his schedule to a Sunday feature and I hope I have the opportunity of meeting him again.

Bill Turnbull and the BBC Breakfast Show – London Calling!

In September 2011 I had my next surprise. I was invited to appear on the BBC Breakfast Show. I had watched the show regularly, often at 6 a.m. from my bed, and having been a fan of the two presenters Bill Turnbull and Sian Williams; I was delighted to have the opportunity of meeting them in the flesh.

Spending a night with friends, I arrived in plenty of time and was taken into the waiting area and then on into the studio. Initially I sat alongside the next person to be interviewed, a BBC presenter of a programme on archaeology. When she took her seat on the sofa, it was obvious she was a professional. I hoped I could do as well. Then it was my turn. After fixing on the mic, the cameraman helped me over a tangled mass of wires to seat on the right-hand side of the red sofa. I was not to meet Sian, but Bill was there. After a few initial words before filming started, which I assumed was to see if I was up to it, while the weatherman read the report, Bill then introduced the subject of the Filter Room and the work of the WAAF. I was relaxed and it was easy to talk. They had managed to take a shot from the Air Ministry film and the whole ten minutes flew by. Returning to the waiting area, I was greeted by another of my favourites, sports presenter Chris Hollins, who had heard the interview and gave me a big hug and a kiss and said, 'Well done!' Almost immediately I was greeted with a gracious nod of the head and a half smile by the dancer-choreographer Craig Revel Horwood as he passed by. I am sorry I left my TV debut so late in life but I had a charming congratulatory email from the producer later in the day.

Following this broadcast, I would meet the producer of an independent film company entitled Impossible Pictures, and after an interview at my home lasting several hours with the producer, I appeared for about three minutes in the fourth of a series of films entitled *Forgotten Heroes*. The screenwriter was the famous Jed Mercurio and he was scheduled to come to my house for the interview but sadly he was a man I did not meet; we spoke over the telephone when the whole interview was conducted remotely.

Shaun Russell and Justin Chaloner – Candy Jar

After my successful campaign to get the drug Lucentis paid for by the NHS in Wales, I was asked to make a video describing a patient's viewpoint when being treated by medical specialists. Two young men arrived to film the interview. This is how I met Justin Chaloner and Shaun Russell. They had joined forces to start their own business. They both had complementary skills: Justin specialising in videography and

Shaun in journalism and PR.

They had learned that I had already published my autobiography through Cardiff University and when they heard I was halfway through *One Woman's War*, they asked to publish it as they had just established a second string to their bow, Candy Jar Books. I was delighted not to have to find an agent and a publisher and I agreed at once. This was when Shaun and Justin became a daily part of my life. A paperback preview copy was published in November 2010 and a hardback followed on my ninetieth birthday with a launch at RAF St Athan. With their varying experience, exciting promotional ideas and a lot of hard work, the results have led to excellent sales but also other interesting activities for me. I have given talks to Bletchley Park veterans, primary school pupils, and the Territorial Army among others. I have also been invited to take part in television and radio programmes, meeting many more interesting people on the way, thanks to their efforts.

I now know much more about these two young men. They both have young families and great ambition, each contributing their unique skills to their enterprise but with entirely different personalities. They continue to make videos and have just completed one of my life, finding incredible wartime footage much of which I had not seen before.

Everyday there seems to be a new chapter opening in the life of this fledging company. It is encouraging to see how tenacity, dedication, hard work and inspiration bring its own reward. I feel rejuvenated seeing a company like Candy Jar spring to life. Entrepreneurs deserve our respect.

Carwyn Jones – First Minister of the Welsh Assembly

My experiences in 1945 at the liberated Breendonk Concentration Camp in Belgium led to my presenting an item during the Holocaust week service in Cardiff City Hall where I would meet for the first time the future leader of the Welsh Assembly, Carwyn Jones. It was a brief meeting but I would later meet him again at the St David's Day celebration dinner in City Hall.

He seemed to remember me, telling me of his interest in Second World War history. I suggested that he might be interested in a film I possessed, recorded during wartime operations in the secret Filter Room. Two years later, when we met again, I reminded him of his promise to visit. In the meantime he had taken over as First Minister of the Welsh Assembly from Rhodri Morgan and was putting his mark on the way devolved Wales was to be governed. As soon as he found room in his calendar, he kept his promise and visited me, accompanied by an aide. We spent an interesting afternoon viewing the film and discussing the history of the Second World War. I found him easy to talk to, despite our differing points of view on politics, and during a subsequent meeting I found him very down to earth.

Prior to his election to the Assembly, Carwyn was a barrister in Chambers in Swansea, specialising in Criminal, Family and Personal Injury as well as being a tutor at Cardiff University Law School. Although I may not agree with his politics, I respect him as a fine, hardworking politician, eager to improve the lives and aspirations of the people of Wales as well as being a most charming man.

John Barrowman and Scott Gill

At the age of ninety-one, I have recently had the opportunity to take tea, drink champagne and converse in an informal way with a multi-talented star, known worldwide. I met John Barrowman: actor, dancer, singer, raconteur and writer. After a starring role in *Doctor Who*, he added to his fame by appearing in *Torchwood* as the hero Captain Jack. The filming took place at the new BBC studios at Cardiff. While based there he found a house on the south coast of Wales between Barry and Penarth in the village in which I live. The view across the Bristol Channel to the coast of Somerset beguiled him and it has become his home, shared with his partner Scott Gill and his bevy of beloved dogs. He calls it his retreat from the many demands on his time and his talents;

a place to chill out.

By chance, one day when visiting a neighbour, Scott noticed a copy of my book on Radar and its secrets. He had apparently intended on buying a copy when visiting Bletchley Park but time did not permit. On learning that the author lived in the village and was a friend of their neighbour, I was invited to call and meet them both. So began what I hope will be a long friendship with two exhilarating companions.

To me, Scott and John are Yin and Yang – opposite characters but who complement each other in a wonderful relationship. To have the privilege of enjoying their company is a bonus and I hope I can add a little colour to their lives. Both are devoted to their families and do so much for charities and causes whenever possible. Seeing how full John's diary is, I am amazed at his stamina. Scott, with his own skills and profession as an architect, brings a stabilising influence to their hectic lives. They make me feel a 'once was' rather than a 'has been'.

Group Captain Tim Willbond – The Dowding System and Brass Hats

My second book *One Woman's War,* dedicated to those in the Women's Auxiliary Air Force, was launched at RAF St Athan on my ninetieth birthday, 4 July 2011, coinciding with the birthday of the then commanding officer, Wing Commander Jones. I was driven around the camp in the special jeep designed for Her Majesty Queen Elizabeth II when she visited Berlin which was shaped like the Pope-mobile. The following week I had the privilege of meeting Group Captain Williams, Air Officer commanding the RAF in Wales during a signing session at the Swansea Air Show.

Things followed fast after the launch and now I am involved with the Association of RAF Fighter Control Officers working on the opening of the museum to be based at the wartime headquarters of Fighter Command at Bentley Priory, Stanmore. It was there Air Marshal Chief Marshal Dowding (known to all as Stuffy) planned the Dowding System. Even now little is known of this vital programme.

Churchill described the wonderful achievement of the Few as a remarkable story of courage and rugged tenacity, saying that their achievement is worthy of the highest and most enduring recognition which they have richly deserved. Less known is that in a further speech he said, 'All the ascendancy of the Hurricanes and Spitfires would have been fruitless but for the system known as the Dowding System. But it is the pivotal role of the Filter Room within that system which allowed commanders at all levels to manage the battle from a common picture of the air.'

Unfortunately this quote has never been given the prominence it so richly deserves but many past and present members of the RAF are now making great efforts to make the public aware of its importance in the history of the Second World War. It is through these efforts that I have come to know Group Captain Tim Willbond, a dedicated retired officer and believer in getting the truth into the public domain. It is now proven that the secret of the Dowding scheme and the work of the seven Filter Rooms in the Second World War should become part of history. He has recently written an official treatise explaining how, without this complicated system of tracking and identifying aircraft approaching our shores, the success of the Battle of Britain and the Battle of London could never have been achieved. This will now be added to the historic annals of the Royal Air Force.

His efforts have reunited some of the remaining WAAF members of the Filter Room, both officers and airwomen, after more than sixty-five years. We have met at the inauguration of Bentley Priory Museum, Stanmore, celebrating the work of Fighter Command and the opening of a commemorative window honouring the young women who worked on Radar and the Dowding System. A further celebration was held in Westminster Abbey on 16 September 2012 during the annual service in memory of the Battle of Britain. As can be imagined, the emotions ran high on both these occasions. His major achievement in bringing to general notice the importance of the Dowding System and the role of the Filter Room will forever be shown in the archives of the RAF since he is writing a paper entitled 'The Filter Centre and its Role and Evolution within the Air Defence Command and Control Structure'.

Lino Scaglioni –A Man with a Civic Conscience

I met Lino Scaglioni after Cardiff University had decided to publish my first book. Other than launch the book, they did nothing else so I was left to find a printer and initiate sales. I was told that the founder of ISIS Printing lived in my village of Sully and that was how I met Lino Scaglioni. It was thanks to him I was led through the intricacies of publishing the first editions of both my books. His help and advice have been irreplaceable. Not only have I learnt a lot about printing books but I have met his family and, I hope, have become a friend. Continuing to work into his eightieth year, he also has instituted a lifeline for the village by inaugurating the lively Sully Residents' Association. We receive regular email communications of everything which may concern the residents; from a lost cat, a problem with local council failings or information about social events and the activities of organisations. Of course we also receive complaints about neighbours, the Vale Council, the police or even someone's barking dog!

Lino combines the charm of an Italian gentleman with the level-headedness of a businessman. In addition to all this he is chairman of the Community Council, a founder member of the Sailing Club and of the Colts football team as well as the inaugurator of the Sully Horticultural Society. He is also active in the village junior and senior cricket clubs. Together with Dorothy, his wife, he works hard both in the factory and also in his immaculate garden where he has his orchid house, another of his hobbies.

His life has had many twists and turns. Born on his grandfather's farm in Grapparrello, Italy, there was no school in this mountainous region. The family emigrated to Britain when he was fourteen and he could neither read nor write. He said that it was from reading the *Beano* and *Dandy* magazines that he eventually mastered these essential arts. As a young man he worked for the P&O shipping line and sailed to Australia and back several times. Following an accident and no longer 'seaworthy', he worked his way up to management with Olivetti, the Italian typewriter manufacturer, in sales. This led to a post in Wales in 1963 where he started a now-extensive family of two sons and a daughter and eight grandchildren.

His contribution to the increasingly pleasant life in this village is immense. His down-to-earth approach to life hides a delightful sense of humour and above all a caring disposition. I am proud to call Lino my friend. And this is the reason for Britain's richness – the gifts that immigrants to these shores bring to enhance our lives.

Paul Cowan – A Master Craftsman

The British Legion has acted as a support through the years to members of the Armed Services and their relatives, providing advice, assistance and care. Within the last ten years a wonderful new service has been available for retired veterans and their wives or husbands. It is called Poppy Calls and it has made a handyman service available throughout the country. These are men with many manual skills, some even with the licence to carry out electric work, and they are each equipped with a van which, when you look inside, is a complete mini-workshop, equipped with tools and equipment to do most type of repair and installation work. It is provided free and even when parts have to be purchased, these too are free. Overall it is a wonderful service, especially for those of us who live on our own.

South Wales was one of the first areas to be provided with this facility and I have been able to use it whenever things needed repairing or installing. Paul Cowan, who was the man delegated to cover my part of South Wales, is a treasure.

Trained and indentured as a cabinet maker and joiner, just like my father, he is able to turn his hand to every sort of job, solving every problem. In addition, in his own free time, he has taken the electrician's training course and now holds the necessary diploma and licence. Nothing has been too much trouble, nothing has been insolvable. Paul has kept everything working in my home and proved a source of help and reliability for the last few years, all in return for just a sustaining cup of tea and an occasional biscuit. Sadly he is now on sick leave, having developed a serious illness. Why do all the good people have to suffer?

Professor John Fairclough – An Orthopaedic Miracle Worker

Like my old car, my chassis is showing signs of wear and my bodywork needs frequent attention. Some years ago after an accident whilst gardening, I had the good luck to become a patient of a very special surgeon. Subsequent disasters have made me realise how lucky and privileged I have been to be under the care of Professor John Fairclough. I now consider him a friend especially as we have the bond of being hispanophiles. We always exchange a few words in Spanish whenever I go to his clinics, much to the consternation of the attendant nurse.

His story is an amazing one. Born in Liverpool, his father was a master butcher and it was from him that John developed an interest in how bodies work. He started with the Christmas turkey and recalls how he would pull it to pieces, analysing the joints and muscles. Together with his siblings, he was encouraged to learn as much as possible from an early age. He decided to go to university to study Medicine and by the age of twenty-three gained his first degree in Medical Science, specialising in Physiology. Two years later he gained his first MB and became a Bachelor of Science.

At Newcastle University he met Sheelagh, who became his wife and a partner in all his efforts. Since she had trained as a geologist, she agreed to marry only as long as he would be prepared to travel, preferably to Africa. He searched for opportunities abroad and received an offer to go to Papua New Guinea – almost as far away from Africa as possible. However the young married couple took up this offer. This remote area at the time had very little medical aid and it meant many people would walk for miles to get to a medical centre. In addition, some of the inhabitants even practised cannibalism! They had many adventures there and despite having then only theoretical, rather than practical experience in both surgery and anaesthetics, John was called upon to undertake both of these tasks on many occasions in order to save a life.

He relates how among the native people, there was a strange sect who had decided one young girl was possessed. They tortured her in order to expel the devil. He managed to rescue her and she had to be taken out of the country for treatment so he escorted her to Britain. Meanwhile, Sheelagh with their new child took sanctuary in a convent awaiting his return.

At the end of the contract he returned to Britain, where although officially not yet trained as a surgeon, his experience was recognised and he was given a surgical post while completing the necessary studies. Within eighteen months he was a fully qualified surgeon. Since then, he has gone on to make his name in both orthopaedic procedures and in sports medicine.

His initial overseas engagement was but one of his many adventures. He has lectured and worked all over the world including in South America, Kuala Lumpa and he is currently visiting India. He has been associated with many publications on medical subjects and made his name when he developed a national and international referral pattern for knee ligaments. In 1988 he was awarded the prestigious Porritt Sports Fellowship. His current research is based on an investigation into the development of osteoarthritis, an affliction more and more current these days. After forty years of service to the National Health, he has recently retired and will now devote himself to researching the causes and effects of osteoarthritis whilst continuing to work with those suffering sports injuries.

He has recently been named by *The Times* as one of our top

surgeons. In addition to all these activities, he manages to find time for several demanding activities including fell running as well as continuing to improve his Spanish. I am both proud and honoured to call him a friend.

Christopher Gorman – The Eyes Have It!

There is another important person who has given me special care. His name is Christopher Gorman. He is a Consultant Ophthalmic Surgeon at the University Hospital Wales, Cardiff and has been the lifeline to keeping the sight in my left eye.

Christopher was born in Lancashire and is not from a medical family. From a very early age he was interested in making and painting the most tiny and intricate Airfix models. Christopher had a childhood interest in history and the Airfix-model making tied well with this. Were the talents he displayed so young – excellent fine motor skills, patience and attention to detail – an early indicator of a future surgeon in the making? While at school he was made to run cross-country and had an alarming difficulty in breathing, his mother took him to the GP who diagnosed asthma and gave him an inhaler which resulted in an immediate improvement in his health. Due to this metamorphosis, he was now to be found right at the front rather than the rear of the cross-country field. The lesson he had learnt from the dramatic transformation in his health and wellbeing due to the use of a simple inhaler made him determined to study medicine and to help other people in a similar way.

Christopher studied Medicine at Leeds. Houseman training was particularly gruelling at that time, regularly requiring more than 110 hours per week but, during this tough training period, comradeship was high and he made lifelong friends with other junior doctors who are successfully practising across the world. As a junior doctor he enjoyed seeing the patient's journey from start to finish and felt a real responsibility for each person under his care. The medical training at

Leeds was comprehensive and well-rounded and he is always appreciative of the wonderful grounding Leeds gave him.

His medical elective was in Fiji and while he was working there a military coup took place. He was arrested and accused of being a spy. He managed to secure his release using his wry sense of humour and by showing his Leeds University library card. Christopher qualified from Leeds with Honours in 1998.

After gaining his degree, Christopher completed his specialist ophthalmic training with a Fellowship at Nottingham's Queens Medical Centre. As part of his supra-specialised training in Vitreoretinal surgery he spent six months in South Africa on an exchange with a Pretorian surgeon. He swapped his house, car and job with Andre. The South African training gave him experience in trauma surgery and volume cataract surgery. He would go out into the country on bush cataract surgery tours with a dedicated team of local doctors and nurses. Patients would walk for days to meet the team. On arrival there would be a hillside full of patients waiting. Christopher explains how sadly, with time and resources so limited, he could triage only the neediest cases for surgery.

When, in 2007, I was diagnosed with wet macular degeneration in my left eye, I learned I could lose my sight unless urgent treatment with a new expensive drug called Lucentis was carried out. I was devastated. I was concerned I would not be able to continue driving, that the second eye might also become affected and that living alone with no close family remaining, my life could become unbearable. I learnt that Lucentis, although not recommended by the National Institute of Clinical Excellence (no doubt based on the very high cost of the drug itself), was already available on the NHS in many places in England and everywhere in Scotland. I felt that this was an injustice, a postcode lottery. Ours is meant to be a *National* Health Service and I had given five years of my life to fighting for my beloved Britain, not randomly selected areas of these Isles. I felt that something must be done.

Speed was of the essence in treating my eye condition. Having some savings available, I decided to pay privately for initial Lucentis injections. At the same time I decided to learn more and to mount a campaign in Wales to persuade the Welsh Assembly that it was inhuman that people in Wales should have to go blind in one eye before treatment was given. I was able to find the money for six initial treatments and had the good fortune through the advice of another doctor to be treated under the care of Christopher Gorman.

At the same time I found out that some of my fellow WAAF service women with no money available for private treatment had already lost their sight. I bombarded Edwina Hart, the Health Minister with emails asking her to investigate the issue. Our correspondence was so prolific that we got to the stage of addressing each other as Eileen and Edwina. At the same time I tackled NICE and the local Health Board.

I gained strong support from the Health Correspondent, a wonderful journalist named Greg Tindle, on the Welsh newspaper, the *Echo*. Greg featured my Lucentis campaign in several editions. The Welsh branch of the Institute for the Blind then became involved and asked for support letters from the public to be sent to lobby the Assembly. Meanwhile the Conservative Health Minister, Jonathan Morgan rallied to the cause and managed to get time in the Assembly for a discussion on the subject. By the time of the Assembly hearing, the pressure had finally made the Labour government in the Assembly change their minds. I was present in the Assembly that day to hear that funding for Lucentis treatment under the NHS had been granted within five clinics around Wales. The very same morning I received a phone call from NICE explaining they had decided that 'not to recommend Lucentis treatment was cruel and inhuman' – success all round!

Chris Gorman's prompt and correct intervention in managing my eye condition undoubtedly saved my sight. Now thanks to the NHS, I continue with my Lucentis injections and under Mr Gorman's watchful eye my sight has been maintained so far. With this treatment and care I maintain my independence, my ability to write, my capability to drive... and to behave... as normally as I am able!

Chris came to Wales in November 2000 and it has been my good fortune to become close friends with his charming and supportive wife Alison and their two endearing daughters Elysia and Sophie. This able surgeon has varied interests and manages to find time for cycling, sailing and keeping fit. However, it is his delight in history and in hearing of my experiences in the Second World War that have given the two of us a very special link.

Aruna Fernando

As an additional bonus I became acquainted with Christopher's Registrar who came to Wales for two years specialist training from Sri Lanka. Another caring man, Aruna Fernando was the first man I have made blush with embarrassment. When I first met him, I was overcome with his beauty – he really had the appearance of a god. I told him he was the most beautiful man I had ever seen. I just couldn't help myself and from that moment we became friends. Aruna recently completed his time in Wales and was due to return home to his family. He joined me for a farewell dinner at my home when I tried to get back to my gastronomic roots and cook a special 'last supper' for him. I still receive reports on his life back home in Sri Lanka.

Ray Price and Gwyn Maguire – My Support Duo – Known as the Groupies

I am frequently requested to visit organisations to talk about the work of the WAAF and specifically the secrets of the Filter Room. The archive film that was uncovered has always been a source of interest but it needs a qualified projectionist to help me display it. Since the venues I go to range from school classrooms to large barren halls, from private houses to museums, I never know what facilities are available but these two very kind men have offered their help. Not only do they escort me to and from the venues but they both possess all the necessary equipment, portable screen, laptop, and projection and amplifying equipment. All I have to do is provide the DVD of the film. Both have held important and responsible posts during their working lives and both are charming companions and excellent drivers. What more could I want?

Ray Price lives in Barry although he is Bristol-born. He has had a varied working life starting out in farming, which led to a period of National Service in the Royal Army Veterinary Corps, including serving in Malaya with the 2nd/7th Ghurkha Rifles. Eventually he trained as a probation officer with a special interest in criminology. He eventually took early retirement from the post of Senior Probation Officer in the Vale of Glamorgan. As one can imagine, his experiences brought him in touch with people of all types, from the very good to the very bad. From my knowledge of him, he is someone always willing to offer help wherever needed.

I first met Gwyn Maguire when I gave a talk to Dinas Powys Probus group and he offered to accompany me to any further talks since he has had a lifelong interest in history. His wife, Rita, seems quite happy to lend him to me for these occasions. He provides all the necessary equipment for showing the film, a portable screen, projection and amplifying equipment and his laptop, ready for any emergency.

His profession was as an engineer, having started at fifteen with apprenticeship training at Llandaff Technical College and the Welsh College of Advance Engineering. This led to employment with Powell Duffryn, initially as a draughtsman but he went on to become a design engineer for equipment used in coal mining, then a mainstay of Welsh industry. He moved on to design and manufacture chemical production equipment for large scale manufacturing plants at home and abroad including nuclear power stations.

A further change saw him employed as a mechanical design engineer for the National Port Authority, involved in all types of maritime engineering and shipping, eventually becoming the South Wales Regional Head of Safety. In the meantime, he studied for a Master's degree in Occupational Health and Safety and Environmental

Management.

How he finds time to spare me an evening now and again I cannot imagine since he belongs to many professional bodies, is doing a course at Cardiff Centre for Lifelong Learning in Italian as well as being keen on DIY. I am sure he is much more than amateur at this since he tells me he built his own house. His ethos is similar to my own, 'It is never too late to learn and there is always something of interest to see and to learn about.' Hear, hear, I say.

With Ray and his experience in criminology and Gwyn in health and safety, I could not have two better guardians in my later years. It is only their cooperation which is allowing me to tell more people about the still little known work of the women of the Women's Auxiliary Air Force.

Robert Towne – Hollywood Knocks at My Door

Who would imagine that at ninety-one years of age, an invitation would be offered to be flown in a Bonanza turbo jet to RAF Duxford for an interview with this famous screenwriter, producer and actor? This happened to me a few weeks after my ninety-first birthday celebrations. It seems that having learned of my WAAF connections, Robert Towne wished to interview me about life in the Air Force as an airwoman and officer and more especially to learn of our relationships with the pilots of Fighter Command. He explained he would be writing a script for a story about the life of a fighter pilot in the highly emotional days of the Battle of Britain. Robert having won an Academy Award for his screenplay for *Chinatown*, is adored by many a screen buff and esteemed by all in the industry.

I have since learned he is the author of many other notable film scripts including the Oscar-nominated screenplay *Shampoo* and the sequel to *Chinatown*, *The Two Jakes* as well as the first two *Mission Impossible* films. On 21 July 2012, I climbed into the co-pilot's seat of the six-seater aircraft, accompanied by the pilot and his wife. Scrambling inelegantly over the wing, I slotted into the seat and adjusted the headset and mike. I was warned to keep my hands off the duplicate set of controls in front of me. It was a wonderful flight over a green and sunny countryside which seemed to be empty of towns, as I listened to the check-ins with air traffic controls at Cardiff, Gloucester, the Mendips, Daventry, Cambridge and finally Duxford. I learned all the special in-talk for checking in and out of the air space – squark numbers for identification and much more. On landing, I was taken to a small darkened room, where I met the iconic Mr Towne. A tall impressive-looking man with a neat beard and smiling eyes, he introduced himself and his colleagues as we had a pre-talk before the filming began. He explained that he and his colleague John Dibbs would ask me questions. He first talked about my experiences in the WAAF. In the room, were a couple of engineers, a cameraman and a young woman holding a microphone as well as Robert's wife and the pilot of the Bonanza.

I was asked questions and told to answer in the form of a statement. I am quite used to that by now, since during the last two years, I have undergone a series of radio, TV and video questionings. So we started. He knew exactly what information he wanted from me and his questions were extremely pertinent. It covered how we met members of the aircrew, how many of the women ended up married to them, how the pilots reacted when they returned from operations, the emotions when the highly paid Americans entered the war, in fact everything possible to give him an accurate idea of the atmosphere of that vital time in our history. Every so often, questions came from others in the room but I was instructed always to remain looking steadily at Robert.

He was painstaking, clear and knew exactly what he wanted. The filming went on for over three hours. He wanted to read a copy of *One Woman's War* to get the atmosphere of a woman's side of the event and was extremely interested in the work of Radar and its effect on the outcome of the battle. He indicated he wanted to include that side of events in the story. When finally we finished the session, he courteously escorted me back to the plane, now quite a distance away on the airfield, and arranged for a wheelchair to help the old girl. He insisted on pushing me himself, escorted by his charming wife. Arriving at the plane, he kissed me goodbye and said he would most certainly be contacting me again. Then with some final gymnastic manoeuvring to get me back in the aircraft, we waved goodbye and I wondered where it would all lead to.

Robert Towne has a fantastic history of association with Hollywood's most famous films. He has been nominated and also won many prestigious awards. I wondered if that would be the end of a brief acquaintanceship. But no, I was soon contacted to ask suitable times for him to phone me. Working out the time difference between California's west coast and the UK, I suggested an evening call between 6 and 8pm would be best, and the first call came a few weeks followed by a further one ten days after that. I am now frequently receiving phone calls from Hollywood, sometimes late in the evening as Robert is working on his script. The filming will be done in the UK and, I have been warned, he will be contacting me even more. This is an intriguing thought and keeps me on my toes, ready and waiting. But the icing on the cake was that as we took off from Duxford, a surprise tribute was being organised and, a few moments after we took off, I was told to look out of the port-side window. To my delight, the Grace Spitfire, with a pupil and his instructor, took off and flew alongside as an escort for about thirty miles, before the pilot opened the cockpit and gave me a wave. As he turned away, he did a victory roll. This took me straight back to the war years, seeing once again the manoeuvre done by our Fighter boys after they had downed an enemy aircraft. The tears came to my eyes with those memories.

John Dibbs

John accompanied Robert Towne and was acting as both advisor and photographer for GK Films when we met. He organised a pilot friend to pick me up in his Bonanza turbo jet at Cardiff airport and also persuaded the pilot of the two-seater Spitfire to give me the thrill of the month by accompanying my departure from RAF Duxford as a fighter escort, culminating in the memory-stirring victory roll. I keep the photo of that Spitfire as my screen saver on my laptop and look at it every day.

John Dibbs has a spectacular reputation for his movie-aviation photography and produces through his company, The Plane Picture Company, an annual diary illustrated with his amazing air pictures. He works with the air forces of many different countries but is primarily based in the USA at Kirkland, Washington State. However, he seemed very interested in my story and asked several very pertinent questions.

'I grew up in north-west London,' John said. 'My father used to watch Spitfires and Hurricanes taking off to fight the Germans as a child. It instilled an interest in him and was passed on to me. I was always interested in aircraft and flight. The actual flying fascinated me as much as the design of the airplane.' He explained that when it was a time to pursue a career, he knew he would have to do something artistic so he has managed to combine that with his love of aircraft.

He served as an apprentice in a London studio as a photographer and graphic designer in the late 1980s, but continued to be fascinated with aircraft and the experiences of pilots and crew in the Second World War. 'I looked at some of the air-to-air photography that was around of restored aircraft and I thought there was a more dynamic way of undertaking that work,' he said. And now he has established a world-wide reputation for his air photographs.

I am looking forward to seeing the outcome of my meeting with these two interesting men when the film – a fictitious tale of pilots during the Battle of Britain – reaches our screens.

Marty Jopson

On Thursday 11th April 2013, I spent nine hours in close proximity with this most talented and entertaining man. The occasion was both interesting and unusual and we spent our time together in decidedly challenging conditions.

Some weeks earlier I had been contacted by a BBC producer who was searching for suitable subjects for the four-minute film slots which appear in the daily BBC One programme entitled *The One Show*. He was interested that during World War Two, while serving as a Filterer Officer at Fighter Command Headquarters, I had been on duty when the Britain experienced the first attack by the V2, the second of Hitler's vengeance weapons.

It was decided to film a mock-up rocket launch by a two-man team of keen rocket modellers, accompanied by a mathematical explanation by me as to how we accomplished the task of tracking the weapons both in the UK and in Belgium. Marty Jopson, a regular presenter on *The One Show* who specialised in science investigations, was given the task of presenting the programme. He had to question me on the mathematics we used to calculate the launch site, using only the pre-computer gadget – a slide rule. It sounded a simple assignment.

Starting around 9 am, we discussed parabolas and their formula, slide rules and their uses while examining a film made in 1943 of the work in the Filter Room. Extracts of both the film and our conversation were filmed successfully and the producer seemed satisfied. At midday we all put on warm jerseys and raincoats and set off to the 'launch site' in a field almost on the border between England and Wales and on the coast of the Bristol Channel. We met the two 'rocketeers' who seemed delighted to meet someone who had been involved with a genuine ballistic missile but by then it was obvious from the darkening skies that April showers would be the order of the day.

As soon as our Land Rover entered the field, we realised how boggy it was. Our driver moved forward cautiously but inevitably we became stuck in the mud. This meant summoning the local farmer to pull us out with his trusty tractor. He seemed delighted and offered to return if we needed him again. We hoped not! Time was marching on. Finally, we were in the correct position to film, about 150 yards from the launch area where one of the rockets were being put into position and fitted with the fuse. We were delighted that the rain had stopped and the sun was shining. Marty and I stood in position to watch and comment on the launch trajectory. The producer gave the order,

'Ready to fire?'

'Yes,' said the rocket man, 'three, two, one, fire!'

Nothing happened.

'The fuse must be wet,' he said.

Time passed as they changed it and the sun disappeared and a slight drizzle started. Yet again the rocket failed to take off. So Marty and I got back in the Land Rover, filmed a short discussion about the use of slide rules while a new more powerful rocket was installed. By this time, the rain had returned and we were interrupted by loud claps of thunder. Finally we managed both a successful launch and appropriate discussion on the event but by then, it was done huddled under a large umbrella in a heavy downpour.

This was not the end. We moved out to the narrow lane, set up again and this time used a model of a V2 rocket complete with its special markings. We stuck it in the soil at an angle and completed the explanation of the mechanism of extrapolation and the mathematics used, with the help of the slide rule. This was not a simple one take – oh no. First there was water on the camera lens, then the sound on Marty's mike failed. Take three appeared to be going well until a large bus turned the corner and drove right through the filming process. Finally at 6pm, a successful take and the usual second one 'for luck' – at last the order came that it was a 'Wrap'. After nine hours our efforts were ready to be edited and cut down to just four minutes on the screen. Who'd be a film star? They must have the patience of saints.

After spending so much time with Marty and sharing the trials and tribulations of the day, I felt we knew each other pretty well. Our mutual sense of humour and tenacity formed a special bond. This is a day I will always remember for its unexpected trials but mutual effort. It was a pleasure meeting you Marty.

Epilogue

I wonder what the future has in store – are there any more interesting men who will stray into my life? I hope so. The panoply of men who have peppered my life so far has changed it from a run-of-the-mill meal to a sumptuous banquet – some dishes more tasty than others! There are men I have loved, men I have loathed, men I have despised and men I have admired. There are ones who taught me, shocked me and amused me. There were some that I was able to teach . But among these men, it is for me to know and you to wonder how many I slept with!

Index of Names